From the High Pennines

The story of an Alderson Family from the 17th Century to the dawn of the 21st.

And of some Bellairs, Bradshaw-Isherwood, Mackenzie, Hodgson and Bland antecedents

Marmaduke Alderson

HAYLOFT

First published 2003

Hayloft Publishing, Kirkby Stephen,
Cumbria, CA17 4EU.

tel: (017683) 42300
fax. (017683) 41568
e-mail: dawn@hayloft.org.uk
web: www.hayloft.org.uk

ISBN 1 904524 07 9

A catalogue record for this book is available
from the British Library

*Cover photograph Jonathan Alderson, courtesy of the Regimental HQ
of the Royal Green Jackets, Winchester*

Produced in Great Britain
Printed and bound in Hungary

Contents

Maps

About the Author

MARMADUKE Alderson was born in Hull in 1939. His first words are said to have been "Go and see lights," a reference to Reckitt's (of Reckitt & Coleman) giant pharmaceuticals factory ablaze following a visit from the Luftwaffe. As a small boy he well remembers walking in a straight line in any direction over cleared bomb sites in the centre of the city, for Hull had been flattened by the blitz and pavements were the long way round.

Marmaduke's father was a doctor whose enormous practice covered much of East Hull. He was a traditionalist in contrast to his mother, who was more of a flamboyant romantic. This clash of cultures resulting in eventual divorce. His mother then rented a large house near York with extensive grounds, lake and woodlands, a paradise for two small boys who enjoyed the outdoor life to the full - bikes, bonfires, boats, donkeys, chickens, pigs, etc. His formal education he describes as "a bit of a shambles" as he was shunted to five different schools in his last five years, and very different kinds of school at that (though all good schools in themselves).

But variety is the spice of life and this gave Marmaduke a colourful view of the world, an insatiable curiosity and the ability to question.

On leaving school he commenced a 38 year career in the aircraft industry, first at Brough in East Yorkshire, then in Montreal, Altlanta and Boston before settling in Bristol, having been attracted there by "the magic of Concorde". He later became a manager of the Airbus programme

Marmaduke became a Bristol City councillor in 1973. He held a range of responsible positions in a 29 year civic career and was Lord Mayor in 1987. He remains actively involved with Bristol's international twinning links, an aerospace museum and local charities. He is also a passionate follower of first class cricket worldwide.

Marmaduke married Karen Sackville-Bryant in 1964 and they have three daughters and two grandchildren.

Illustrations

Preface

When I was a boy my father and grandmother were continually talking about our family history but being younger and wiser, my brother and I preferred the outdoor life of climbing trees, lighting bonfires or doing civilised things such as playing cricket in the garden. I was nineteen when my father died and I inherited his old medical bag, for he was a doctor. But it did not contain medical paraphernalia but rather a pile of scrap books and papers. It was safely put away and not seen again for another 20 years.

When it was eventually opened up, a treasure trove of Victorian family photographs, notes and press cuttings was discovered from which a family tree of several generations was easily compiled. At about the same time I re-discovered my godfather, Christopher Alderson Howes-Smith, and from him, a third cousin once removed, came a veritable flood of information embellished with real meat on the bone, for Christopher had lived all his life on the Yorkshire-Derbyshire border, an important part of the country to the Aldersons. I was hooked.

I have since collected a considerable amount of information but my children are about as interested as I was as a boy, so what to do with it, I pondered? Rather than risk it all being lost I would put pen to paper and thereby place it securely on the record.

I am a founder member of the Alderson Family History Society but have done little to support the excellent and professional work that has been achieved. The Society, however, has helped me, supplying factual information gleaned from many a Record Office or Reference Library and I am grateful to them, and in particular to Susan Sharp, for many years Record Officer and Projects Co-ordinator. On 5 November 1991 Susan suggested that I write an Alderson biography. She has supplied much of the information on the early Alderson years in Swaledale and Westmorland and has been a constant source of encouragement for which I am most grateful.

I have received considerable support from my third and second cousins, both once removed, Anne Maier and Chris Cottier respectively, the former particularly for information on the Mackenzie line and the latter for the South African and 20th century Canadian connections.

I have tried to be accurate and to quote sources but it is necessary to employ an element of free rein to flesh out some of the more interesting characters. I hope it is clear when opinion replaces fact.

I have started with the earliest known Alderson ancestors and have progressed chronologically, except when crossing into the distaff side. Here it has sometimes seemed logical to go in reverse order. To help readers follow the flow, refer to the family tree at the rear of the book, which quotes the paragraph number that relates to the main characters. When laterals have a particular story to tell, I have most often included them with their siblings, rather than with their parents, to keep the generations together. In such cases I have inserted a line into the text.

I may be accused of name dropping, but people in the public eye are more likely to have had their activities recorded and hence available for re-use. There have been persistent family rumours that John Flamsteed, the first Astronomer Royal, and a 17th century Mayor of Chester, are ancestors, but evidence has not been forthcoming so both are omitted.

Some county boundaries were changed in 1974. Sedbergh, for example, was transferred from Yorkshire to the newly created Cumbria, which also absorbed the whole of Westmorland which, regrettably, no longer exists. I have used the old boundaries as they were current at the time.

I hope readers derive pleasure from reading this story.

Marmaduke Alderson,
"Gannow," Bristol.
February 2003

1

The High Pennines

Yorkshire is a county of contrasts. Within its broad acres lie great cities of the industrial revolution and pretty market towns, ports which trade with the world and small fishing villages, magnificent cathedrals and medieval village churches, great country houses with their parks overlooking wold and dale and by contrast boggy windswept moors. The wildest and most rural of these moors, wilder even than those used to dramatic literary effect by Charles Dickens and Emily Brontë, was home to the early Aldersons.

Most Aldersons who research their family line eventually arrive in Upper Swaledale, the bleakest of the dales, with a haunting, ethereal beauty in the far north western corner of Yorkshire, or perhaps just over the county boundary into County Durham or Westmorland. These are the High Pennines, offering some of the finest scenery in Britain. They are rolling treeless hills occupied by a vast army of disinterested sheep, with all the colours of nature reflected in the occasional mountain tarn. In the lower reaches they are divided by carefully crafted dry stone walls, interspersed by the occasional lonely farmstead with a few bullocks reared in the home pasture.

In these Pennine hills a straggly string of tiny becks rise to start their journey to the sea. Those in Yorkshire flow to the east and the River Swale, through Richmond to join the Ure, then the Ouse and finally into the Humber and the North Sea. Those in Westmorland flow westwards into the River Eden, then northward to Carlisle and via the Solway Firth into the Atlantic.

The inhabitants of these moors and dales lived modest lives in the 17th century, mostly as shepherds or as lead or coal miners. The men often knitted to augment their incomes as they walked across the fells to the mines; today the area is littered with disused mine workings.

In the late 18th and 19th centuries, many dales' inhabitants moved to the expanding cities of the West Riding, Northumberland, Co. Durham and Lancashire, as part of the great migration of the industrial revolution,

The High Pennines

and others emigrated to the four corners of the Empire. Our story takes us to South Africa, Canada, Jamaica, Gibraltar, Bechuanaland and Panama, and touches on Northern Rhodesia, Ceylon, New Zealand, India, Brazil and The United States of America. It eventually deposits us at the beginning of the 21st century, thirteen generations and nearly 400 years from its beginnings, and on the way takes us up other lines of direct ancestry back to the first millennium.

The origin of the Alderson name is far from certain and arouses considerable debate amongst scholars. The simplest explanation is that it is derived from "son of Aldred." Another is that it comes from Aldehous, which means old house in medieval Scandinavian languages, and that the son was added as a patronymic, giving Aldehousson. Plantagenet Harrison's unsubstantiated pedigree of 1154 commences with "Aldoue de Bolton, co, Lancaster, a vassal of William de Vescy, Sheriff of Lancaster." His son is William Aldouesson of Bolton and his sons took the surname Alderson - though not related to my family, one must add.

Alderson was the most common name in Upper Swaledale. A list of fifty tenants in 1538 had among them seventeen Aldersons, followed by eight Metcalfes, eight Milners and six Harkers. A century and a quarter later a list of 106 petitioners contained twenty Aldersons, eighteen Milners, eleven Harkers and seven Metcalfes.

Overlooking Whitsun Dale on Ravenseat Moor, a mile south of the Yorkshire Westmorland county border, is Alderson Seat.

2

Simond of Muker

Our story starts in the early 17th century when we find Simond Alderson, who I believe to be my eight greats grandfather (we all have 512 of them remember), living in Muker in Swaledale. The Muker parish registers tell us that Simond had three sons, Simond who was baptised on 19 May 1639, Richard of Butt House on 21 February 1641 and John on 11 November 1645.

Half a century later, in 1688, the year of the "Glorious Revolution" and the last of the reign of James II, a dispute came into the Exchequer about the tithes that should have been paid by the inhabitants of the Parish of Grinton in Swaledale, which included Muker. The plaintiff was Tobias West, Clerk of Grinton, and the many defendants included no less than 25 Aldersons. "Depositions by Commission" were taken in Kirkby Stephen in Westmorland from which the following extracts are found:

"Richard Alderson of High Ubank upon Stainmore, Collyier, aged 48 or thereabouts sworn and examined deponeth that it is about 20 years since he lived in Keld in the Parish of Grinton and that he had lived about 30 years in the said parish...."

"Simon Alderson of Swaledale in the County of York, yeoman aged 49 years and upwards...."

"John Alderson of Hardrigge Head in the parish of Grinton aged about 42 years."

High Ubank, now High Ewebank the Ordnance Survey tells us, is in Westmorland, close to the county boundary with Yorkshire.

The names from the Kirkby Stephen Depositions are identical to the three sons of Simond of Muker and the birth dates and ages are almost a perfect match. Thus Richard Alderson, who I believe to have been my seven greats grandfather, was born in the parish of Muker, almost certainly in Keld in upper Swaledale in Yorkshire, and moved across the county boundary to Westmorland in about 1658 when he would have been seventeen years old.

Swaledale was settled variously by Scandinavians, who invaded from Ireland in 700-900AD, by Celts, by Norsemen, by the visiting Romans who developed the lead mining industry, by Saxons and by the Normans following the Conquest. Keld is a tiny cluster of greystone houses and cottages, Muker a rather larger village, and both are flanked by the River Swale in its upper reaches and are protected by the grandeur of the Pennines which rise steeply above them.

Muker, a name of Norse derivation meaning narrow cultivated acre, was part of the parish of Grinton until the 19th century and was the centre of social life in upper Swaledale. Keld, a further three miles up river, was originally a Saxon settlement, its name coming from the old Norse word for a well or a spring.

The subject of the dispute under investigation was failure to pay the full level of tithes to the vicar of Grinton, some of the sheep having been spirited away to reduce their numbers at the critical time. It throws an interesting light on 17th century life in the dales. It appears from the various testaments that "every parishioner that keepeth any sheepe in the said parish on Monday, Tuesday, Wednesday next after midsomer day each yeare bring in all their lambes to the most usuall and convenient tything places within the severall townes and hamletts of the said parish most proper for the speedy tything the same and respectively pay to the vicar and Impropriator."

Widow Agnes Alderson, it appears, no relation of mine, rest assured,

Muker in Swaledale

11

"did to trouble the defendant in collecting his tythe remove her lambs to a sheepfold more remote and further distant than the former sheepfold where the lambs used to be tythed before."

A tythe being a tenth part, we learn of the custom pertaining to flocks of fewer than ten lambs. "... every parishioner that is but only possessed of eight lambs at the tytheing thereof usually taketh up only one and the Vicar and Impropriator then take their tythe Lamb out of the remainder." When only "seaven" lambs it appears that the vicar had first choice from the flock, if only five lambs then a price is agreed for the best lamb and lotts are cast to decide who has the lamb and who then pays the other party half that price and if the poor parishioner had only four lambs, then he paid the vicar a penny for each one. The formula for a flock of six lambs does not receive a mention and neither do we know the fate of naughty Widow Alderson!

3

High Ewebank
Richard, William and Jonathan Alderson

In contrast to the shelter afforded by the steep slopes of the dale of the Swale, High Ewebank is on high ground in eastern Westmorland on windswept Stainmore. It was never more than a hamlet, its heyday probably having been in the 18th century. The 1787 census shows ten families living there, three Aldersons, two Oystons, two Moores, a Grisedale, a Holiday and a Preston. The occupations of the heads of households were husbandry, miner or labourer and in most cases they were supported by wives and daughters listed as "knitting." In total the population was 51 people, the Alderson families being the largest.

A century later the population was substantially reduced, the 1881 census listing only three residents remaining. There was just one inhabitant in 1994, a Mrs Brown, a hardy soul who would trudge the seven miles to Kirkby Stephen for groceries, but even her house looked empty and forlorn two years later. Perhaps High Ewebank should now be added to the list of England's deserted villages.

One of the oldest Stainmore names is Ewebankes, which goes back to the dark ages, and has given rise to the legend of Stainmore's Headless Woman. A local marauding chieftain in Saxon times was called Dew Bank, whose fort was possibly near the current High Ewebank. These fells were a good hunting ground for stag, grouse and wild boar. One one occasion Dew Bank's hunting party met that of the Norman baron, Fitz-Barnard and they quarrelled over hunting rights and a skirmish ensued, Dew Bank having the better of the engagement. He captured Fitz-Barnard's beautiful daughter, Ethel, as prisoner and took her to his impregnable fort. But Dew Bank fell in love with the Ethel, treated her kindly and asked her to marry him. Ethel refused. Eventually, with the help of Ralph de Neville's men an expedition set forth to rescue her. In the furious fighting that ensued Ethel fled on a bay horse and galloped away for her life. Enraged at the loss of his loved one, Dew Bank, in a blind anger, chased after her and with one mighty stroke of his sword

High Ewbank, Westmorland

severed her head. To this day, so Stainmore folk will tell, Ethel may still be seen at the midnight hour, on a grey charger, her blue dress billowing behind her, as she gallops across Stainmore towards Barnard Castle.

Westmorland was a small county and, with Cumberland, parts of north Lancashire and westerly pieces of Yorkshire, was subsumed into the newly created county of Cumbria in the local government reorganisation of 1974. However appropriate this might have been in geographical terms one should not suppose there to have been similarities in all fields; indeed, the very opposite was often the case.

There was a strong yeomen tradition in Westmorland. The county contained many small freehold farms, the farmers themselves owning the land. These men were proud of their small estates and it bred a fierce independence of mind and spirit, in contrast to other northern counties where great estates were to be found, farmed by men who were little more than serfs to their absentee noble lord.

In Westmorland the land passed down to the elder son and heir but younger sons had also to be provided for. The army or the church were the traditional routes open to them but a sound education was a necessary prerequisite for advancement. Needs must, and Westmorland developed a fine tradition of excellence in its schools. In 1825, Lord Brougham, then Lord Chancellor, in a speech in the House of Lords, stated that the standard of education in Westmorland was second only in Europe to that in Switzerland.

Perhaps it was this tradition of learning that led to Michael Faraday, whose family came from Wrenside, a hundred yards across the River Belah from High Ewebank, becoming the great physicist and chemist and the discoverer of electromagnetic induction and the laws of electrolysis.

Kirkby Stephen is five miles to the west of High Ewebank and Yorkshire no more than two miles to the south-east. There are magnificent panoramic vistas of the Pennines in all directions with hardly a building in sight but rather lush green fields, dry stone walls and sheep, sheep and more sheep. The view is so spectacular it was called "The Plains of Heaven" by the Victorian painter John Martin. The River Belah flows in the small dale to the west and Stainmore stretches to the east and into County Durham. The remnants of a disused railway line lay a mile to the north. Nearby Brough-under-Stainmore, on the old high road from London to Glasgow, occupies the site of the ancient Veteris, where, towards the decline of the Roman Empire in Britain, a prefect with a band of directores was stationed. Brough flourished as a place of considerable importance prior to the Conquest, but the northern English did not take kindly to change and conspired against King William, the usurper. The King, however, as Kings usually do, had the last laugh.

Returning to our story we see from the parish registers of Brough that Richard Alderson of Eubanke married Ann Waller on 9 June 1664. He would then have been 23. They had a son Simond baptised on 17 May 1665 and a second son William baptised on 10 March 1667. I believe William to be my six greats grandfather.

On 31 July 1693, when William would have been aged 26, he married Elizabeth Grumwell and in all likelihood would have continued to live at High Ewebank. William was buried on 1 January 1698/9 at Brough.

The Westmorland Rentals of Lord Thanet's Estate tell us that from 1749 to 1755 a Jonathan Alderson paid rent of £3 for Margaret Grumwell's tenement at High Ewebank. Margaret is most likely to have been Elizabeth Grumwell's daughter by her second marriage, her marriage to William Alderson having lasted only six years. Thus this Jonathan would have been Margaret's half brother and hence the son of William Alderson and Elizabeth Grumwell. Jonathan's baptism has not been found but this supposition makes him my five greats grandfather.

Jonathan Alderson married Elizabeth, née Alderson, on 8 January 1706/7. That Jonathan and Elizabeth were my five greats grandparents is not in doubt but if this Jonathan was indeed the son of William Alderson and Elizabeth Grumwell then he would have been thirteen years old when he married or alternatively would have been born prior to his parents' marriage. The evidence points to it being the correct link but perhaps there has to be one conundrum in a good story. How much easier life would be if genealogy were a science of certainties.

Jonathan Alderson and the Grumwells appear to have been involved in mining; we have seen above that his grandfather Richard was a collier. A letter watermarked 1826, written by a John Alderson to H P Pulleine , tells us:

Honoured Sir,

I have sent you an account of what the old writings spacifyes concerning the working of Taylor Rigg and the Low Pitt which was begun by James and Thomas Grumwell from Durham in the year 1604 which theay brought awater Level drift out of Easegill which laid the high part of the colliery dry to the south east end of Taylors Rigg which extends into your Liberty after that it fell into the hands of Messrs Goss and Ewebank who wone it of alower Derection with awater Injen. After that it came into the hands of John Alderson who lived at High Ewebanke and we have sume Old Bookes of his which gives ous this Account a great Dike which cuts the Coale of cumes of the Bants side and on the East side of thare Eanjen pitt which theay are at present working which stands by the side of Easegill which runs 80 yeards north east of an old shaft which is in your Liberty that goes by the name of Hollidays shaft which on the point of the compass is 274. Likewise the point of the greate Dike runs at the point of 45 this is all the account I have respecting Taylors Rigg.

I rinaine your most obdent and Humble servant,

JOHN ALDERSON.

John Alderson, the author of this statement, was likely to have been a descendant, most probably a grandson, of Jonathan Alderson of High Ewebank.

Taylor Rigg and Ease Gill are three miles south east of High Ewebank, almost at the meeting point of Westmorland, Yorkshire and County Durham. Evidence shows that Pulleine was involved in other mine leases in the immediate vicinity, one in 1732 involving a Christopher

Alderson, though no link to Jonathan Alderson is known. Neither is it known how well Jonathan fared with these business ventures, but it may be the clue to the prosperity that was to be the good fortune of at least one of his sons in later years.

4

Elizabeth Alderson
And the Bible boys of keld

Elizabeth Alderson was born at Muker in Swaledale, the daughter of Christopher Alderson and Anne Cooper. A statement has been found attesting that she and Jonathan were cousins but this is countermanded by a statement to the contrary. The contrary statement is believed.

Elizabeth's marriage confirms that contact had been maintained between Muker and Keld in Swaledale and High Ewebank in Westmorland. Though only ten miles apart, this could not be taken for granted in the early 18th century. High Ewebank would have looked to Kirkby Stephen as its local market town and Muker in the opposite direction to Richmond. The route between the two would have been via Tan Hill, home to the highest pub in Britain and transport would have been either on horseback or foot, a tortuous journey today over rough roads, steep hills and hairpin bends, yet more so in the 18th century.

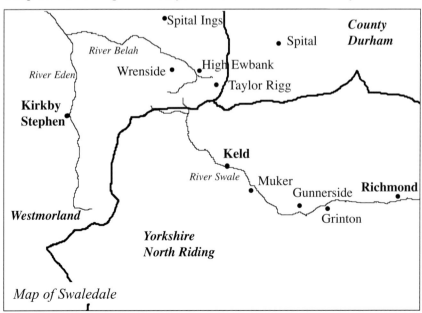

Map of Swaledale

Elizabeth's father, Christopher Alderson, was the youngest son of John Alderson of Keld. John, who was living in 1675, had bought a Bible in York in 1638 and entered the names of his six sons in it, viz. Miles, Edmund, Anthony, William, George and Christopher. John in turn was the son of Miles Alderson of Keld, a tenant of Lord Wharton in 1618.

Miles Alderson lived in Keld at about the same time that Simond lived in Muker. They were the respective great grandfathers of Elizabeth Alderson and Jonathan. Being so close, one presumes that they knew each other, but it is far from certain that they were related due to the prevalence of the Alderson name in Swaledale.

The marriage between Jonathan and Elizabeth was a fertile one, for between 1727 and 1752 Elizabeth gave birth fourteen times; to Mary, Elizabeth, David, George, Ann, Jonathan, Christopher, William, William again, John, Thomas, Richard, Robert and Joseph. All were baptised at Stainmore Chapel, a Chapel of Ease to the church of Brough-under-Stainmore. Elizabeth died in giving birth to Joseph, who himself lived for three months only and was buried on Christmas Eve in 1752. William the elder and Robert also died young.

Christopher, the fourth son and seventh child of Jonathan and Elizabeth Alderson of High Ewebank, was my four greats grandfather and from here the story becomes based more on certainty than surmise.

There are a number of known living descendants of others from among this clutch. Among them is Bernard Alderson of Pennsylvania, who descends from Christopher's brother, Richard and his wife Esther Ashton.

5

Christopher "Gardener" Alderson
Rector of Aston and Eckington

Christopher Alderson, was baptised at Stainmore Chapel on the 4 August 1737. Most of his brothers became shepherds or miners but Christopher's future was to be different, very different indeed. He was educated at Sedbergh and Cambridge, entered the Established Church, was befriended by gentry and royalty and was granted arms. He became a very wealthy man.

The bald facts are (bearing in mind contradictory information among some of the records) that Christopher was ordained deacon at Chester on 21 September 1760, priest on 6 September 1761 and became curate of Howgill in Yorkshire in the same year. He was rector of Langton-on-Swale from 1768-77, rector of Eckington in Derbyshire from 1784-1814, vicar of Drayton and Askham in Nottinghamshire in 1772 and of Tickhill in Yorkshire from 1775-7. He was vicar of Wadsworth in Yorkshire in 1778 and Rector of Oddington in Gloucestershire from 1779-85. He was curate at Aston in Yorkshire for many years and became rector in 1797, a position he held until 1811.

What was it that led Christopher away from the windswept moors of the High Pennines to the lush pastures of the wealthy crown livings of Aston and Eckington? One may only surmise, but perhaps the Westmorland tradition of hard work and learning had played its part.

Christopher almost certainly attended the Free School in Stainmore. The school had been built in 1594 with the help of Sir Cuthbert Buckell, a son of Stainmore, who became Lord Mayor of London in 1593 and was a freeman of the Vintners Company.

Having made his fortune, Dick Whittington style, Buckle remembered his native county by founding a chapel and by endowing a school "… for the performance of divine service and the education of children in religion and good manners," and by his last will and testament of 24 June 1594 bequeathed £8 a year out of his estates called "le Spittel upon Stainmore" for the perpetual support of a chaplain and schoolmaster."

The Spittle name is still to be seen, with spelling variations, on the Ordnance Survey, running east from High Ewebank into County Durham alongside the River Greta.

The chapel was consecrated by Bishop Henry in 1600. In the course of time "...due to weather and the carelessness of the trustees the structure ran to decay and was ready to fall to ruin." At this point Thomas, Earl of Thanet, "took compassion" and not only repaired the chapel but also built a school house close by in 1699 "...at the expense of above £100. By a Deed Tripartite betwixt him and his heirs, 12 of the principal inhabitants of the place and the Bishop of Carlisle did settle and secure an annual rent and revenue of £12 issuing out of his lands for the better and more laudable support of the curate and schoolmaster forever. Within the bounds of this Chappelry, are reached the village of High Ewebank of 12 families and about six scattered houses every one of which has its different and distinct name. In 1720 the pious and generous Lord gave £200 more to this Chappel and thereby procured £200 from the Commissioners and Trustees of Queen Anne's Bounty to the poor clergy." Thus reported the Rev Todd in his manuscript of 1720.

Christopher was intelligent and presumably responsive, and thus would have been noticed by the schoolmaster, who was also the local curate and who took divine service on Sundays. The curate would

The Old School, Sedbergh

21

discuss the potential of his pupils with his vicar, and as the landlord at High Ewebank in Christopher's day was the Earl of Thanet, it is likely that this was the route to his preferment. Christopher might also have had a helping hand from a new prosperity generated by his father for, as mentioned earlier, there are hints that Jonathan had became involved in developing the mining industry.

From the Sedbergh School records we learn that Christopher entered the school some time between 1746 and 1760, when he would have been between the ages of nine and 23. This tells us that he was destined for the Anglican Church.

There would have been fewer than 40 pupils at Sedbergh during Christopher's time and it was a very different place from the school of today. The "old school" still exists, a single solid rectangular building with a slate roof looking more like a nonconformist chapel and the conditions would have been spartan.

The headmaster during Christopher's years was Wynne Bateman, a man of energy and force of character. He was highly skilled both as a classical scholar and as a teacher of mathematics and the triumph of Sedbergh boys in these subjects made the school famous at Cambridge. One of Bateman's

Aston Church

little vanities was to preach a Latin sermon before the University which he would afterwards publish. Perhaps as a counter balance to his scholastic intellect, he was also interested in magic and the black arts!

Christopher was 34 years old when he was admitted to Pembroke College, Cambridge on 16 October 1771 as a "ten year man," a mature student, and as a sizar, a student receiving an allowance from the college. He was awarded his

Bachelor of Divinity in 1782.

In one particular, Christopher left his mark at Cambridge, for it is believed that the inscription "Old Alderson," carved in bold letters on a wooden pew in the Pembroke College Chapel, Wren's first ecclesiastic commission, relates to him.

It was almost unique for a boy from the High Pennines to become ordained but his second break was equally audacious, for in 1767 Christopher married Elizabeth, daughter of William Ball, steward to the Holderness family. More particularly, they were married at Aston in South Yorkshire and it was here and in nearby Eckington that he was to live for the rest of his long life. Aston is 100 miles south of Swaledale and is a very different part of this large county: lush pastureland compared to the weather beaten northerly parishes of Howgill and Langton-on-Swale.

Christopher became curate at Aston to William Mason, the "Parson's Poet," and eventually succeeded him as Rector on the presentation of the Duke of Leeds, to whom the manor had passed following the death of the fourth Earl of Holderness.

William Mason (1724-1797), poet, artist, author, musician and critic was the son of the vicar of Holy Trinity, Hull. His grandfather had been collector of customs at Hull and his great grandfather sheriff in 1675 and mayor in 1681 and 1696.

Mason was a graduate of St John's College, Cambridge, though later he was elected fellow of Pembroke, thanks to the pressure of his friend Thomas Gray. In 1749 he had been employed to write an ode to the Duke of Newcastle to celebrate his becoming Chancellor of Cambridge University. In 1754 he was presented by Robert D'Arcy, fourth and last Earl of Holderness, to Aston. Here he built the parsonage house.

Alderson was curate to Mason for upwards of 25 years, yet this did not retard his opportunities elsewhere. Eckington is just four miles away across the county boundary in Derbyshire, and for fourteen years he was rector of Aston and Eckington in plurality. Thus he was able to maintain his close relationship with Mason, whilst also having his own parish and the tithes that derived from this other wealthy Crown living.

After Mason's death in 1797 Christopher succeeded as rector of Aston or more fully, Aston with Aughton, (Aston - the settlement amid the oak trees and Aughton - the settlement amid the ash trees), a position he held until 1811. The Reverend George Kirk, who became rector of Aston in

1956, in his book of the church described the Aldersons as a typical wealthy and conscientious clerical family.

There has been a church at Aston since AD 700. At the time of the Domesday survey the village was known as Estone and was recorded as being of arable, pasture and woodland with a value of eight shillings.

Among Mason's friends was Thomas Gray and it is believed that it was in the summer house of Aston Rectory that Gray wrote his *Elegy in a Country Church Yard*.

Eckington was a large parish in Christopher's day, embracing parts of what is now an expanded Sheffield, but it has since been split many times. The glebe was plentiful, providing sufficient income to enable Alderson to have at least three curates, (one of whom was later to get a living in Yarmouth and find a lady worth £100 a year!). Christopher built the fine rectory at Eckington, the size of the rooms showing it to have been designed for entertaining. The last rector noticed the upstairs corridor to be 22 yards long, so one wonders if the summer game was transferred indoors on rainy days! The rectory was only abandoned by the Church in the early 1990s, when it was finally sold to the current inhabitants.

Eckington was an important centre for the manufacture of scythes and sickles which were sold in every part of the British Isles and exported to America, Russia and Poland.

November 5th had a particular significance for the people of Eckington. In the vestry is a prayer book dating from 1683 which Alderson used. It contains a prayer for use on 5 November for "the happy deliverance of the King .... from the most Traitorous and Bloody intended Massacre by Gunpowder!" More significantly to many parishioners, a statute fair was held in Eckington, also on 5 November, for the hiring of servants. The sequence in which these two events occurred is not specified.

We hear today of people living to be a hundred but this must have been rare indeed in the 18th century, particularly for a man. Such an occasion occurred at Killamarsh, in the parish of Eckington, and Alderson had it duly recorded on a large tablet which may still be seen on the outer wall of Killamarsh Church. It reads:

To the Memory of John Wright, a pauper of this parish, who died May 4th 1797 in the 103rd year of his age. He was temperate and cheerful and in the trying situation of darkness, poverty and old age, bore his

Eckington Rectory with the church spire visible behind.

infirmities with such Christian meekness as executed the benevolence of good men and is here recorded as an instructive lesson to others.

Rev. Christopher Alderson, B.D., P.P.P.
AD 1797 30 years Rector of Eckington with Killamarsh.

In 1789 Eckington welcomed a new arrival, six year old Augusta Byron, the elder half sister to the poet and daughter of Mad Jack Byron and Amelia, Baroness Conyers, and there was scandal in the air. Amelia was the daughter of the fourth and last Earl of Holderness on whose death she had inherited title and wealth. In 1773 she had married Francis Godolphin Osborne, the Marquess of Carmarthen and heir to the Duke of Leeds. The Rev. Christopher Alderson had officiated, the wedding taking place at Holderness House.

Amelia did her duty and bore Carmarthen two sons but she then entered headlong into a passionate and reckless love affair with Mad Jack Byron. Amelia stayed in London whilst her husband was away in Bath or Hornby and both she and Mad Jack took the opportunity afforded them with open arms, eschewing discretion entirely but rather flaunting the affair. The Marquess, on learning of this, was not amused and in 1779 divorced his wife. Amelia was by then heavily pregnant. She and Mad Jack married immediately and again Christopher Alderson officiated. This time the wedding was at Hanover Square, where a few decades earlier Handel had regularly played the organ. Very much a high society wedding this would have been, albeit between the "black sheep" of their respective families.

The baby was born shortly after the wedding but died soon afterwards. It was to be another three years before Amelia became pregnant again but on 26 January 1783 Augusta Mary, was born. It had been a difficult birth from which Amelia never wholly recovered and on 26 January 1784, on Augusta's first birthday, she died.

Father Mad Jack was nowhere to be found, probably pre-occupied with his chums hunting and shooting, so it was to grandmother Lady Holderness that responsibility for baby Augusta fell. After the baby's first years Lady Holderness sought a more suitable home for a growing child, a homely household where she would be brought up in the fear of God, and a home where she would be safe from the clawing fingers of Mad Jack, interested more in the wealth that would be Augusta's, rather than drawn by any paternal instinct.

Christopher Alderson was just the man. For the past sixteen years he had been chaplain to the Holderness family and since the Earl's death had been a close and trusted friend to Lady Holderness, advising her on legal and financial matters. Furthermore, Eckington was off the beaten track, tucked away in the southern Pennines, and a safe distance from the main arteries of 18th century England.

Elizabeth Alderson, the rector's wife, gave Augusta a warm welcome to Eckington, which became her home for seven years. This was a happy time for Augusta who enjoyed, perhaps for the only time in a long life, peace and tranquillity as she settled into the day to day activities of a country parson's household. Mary, the Alderson's youngest child, was the same age as Augusta and became a soul-mate and a lifelong friend.

It was certainly not from Eckington that Augusta was set on her wayward spiral towards an incestuous relationship with her half brother and into a disastrous marriage with her reckless cousin, George Leigh, gambler, womaniser and swindler. On learning of Elizabeth Alderson's death in 1817 Augusta described her "as a mother to me... who ... loved me so well." In 1819 Augusta was visited by Mary in her Grace and Favour apartment at St James' Palace. During her month long stay they spent many happy hours reminiscing about a shared and happy childhood at Eckington.

Byron was a fifteen year old school boy at Harrow when he first met Augusta, tall, graceful, five years his senior and strikingly beautiful. He was immediately attracted to her.

Byron had married Annabella Milbanke, one of Augusta's closest friends, but to all intents and purposes the marriage lasted barely a month. Thereafter Annabella was constantly humiliated by Byron. He would order his wife to bed, who would then have to endure the sounds from below of him flirting with Augusta, the two of them giggling and having a merry time, Augusta barely attempting to withstand Byron's advances. That Byron and his half sister had an incestuous relationship is not in doubt. They were madly, passionately in love, this the one true love of the great poet and womaniser's life. Augusta had seven children, all officially by her husband George Leigh, but there is reason to suppose that the penultimate child, Medora, was sired by Byron.

In 1814 Byron, the 6th Lord, took Augusta to his "seat," Newstead Abbey in Nottinghamshire. It was in a sad state and was shortly to be sold to pay off debts but at the first sight of the ancestral home of both of them, Augusta was spellbound, describing herself as "a child of this place." Thereafter she described Newstead as "our dear old Abbey." She and Byron carved their names on a tree in the grounds.

Reviewing some other of Christopher's parishes tells us that he rebuilt the parsonage house whilst vicar of Tickhill in South Yorkshire. He was able to place his eldest son, Jonathan, at nearby Harthill and secured

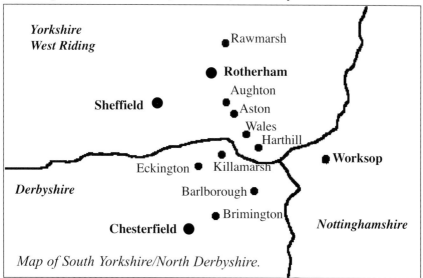

Map of South Yorkshire/North Derbyshire.

Aston for his second son William in succession to himself. He was given the advowson - the right of presentation to the benefice - of the living of Kirkheaton near Huddersfield. The odd parish out was far away Oddington, in Gloucestershire, but the rectorship was in the gift of Mason, as Precentor of York Minster. In 1768, a decade prior to him becoming rector there, Mason had told Alderson "If the Bishop asks you anything about Oddynton you will say that you know nothing about it.." A search through the parish registers has found no entries under Alderson's name so it is safe to assume that he hardly ever, if at all, visited Oddington, though no doubt he was pleased to take the parish tithes.

Throughout his years at Aston and Eckington Christopher maintained an interest in the welfare of his brothers, involved as they were with shepherding and lead mining and probably also coal mining at the King Pit, close to their original home of High Ewebank. He paid the rent for Wrenside, adjoining High Ewebank, at least between 1773 and 1775, which was the home of his brother Jonathan and family, and then of his brother Richard, this the Wrenside that had once been the home of the Faraday family.

Between 1767 and 1769, and possibly for longer, Jonathan and his brother George were living at North Park House in the parish of Hornby, referred to again in the next chapter. Christopher was also in touch with his younger brother Thomas whilst at Aston.

Christopher Alderson had a great love of gardening. His green fingers and natural eye for time and space were at one with the new English landscape style, as his fine parsonage gardens bore witness. A quarter of a millennium later many remain as fully matured gardens, often still sporting his hallmark, the copper beech. That at Killamarsh was chopped down in the 1980s, but those at Harthill and Eckington remain. Eckington is perhaps the best existing example of one of Christopher's gardens, where in late spring his copper beech may still be seen in fresh leaf and full majesty. There is also an acacia tree that Alderson planted which still flowers, despite having suffered recent storm damage. The acacia is a North American specimen and was brought to Europe by the French. It is claimed in Eckington that Christopher imported his acacia from Italy and that it was the first in England.

Mason was confidant and correspondent to Horace Walpole, the son of the former Whig prime minister, and the great arbiter of taste. W S Lewis, the editor of Walpole's papers, states that Mason "shows Alderson a paternal affection." This is confirmed by the way Walpole signed letters to Alderson. "God bless you and make you happier than I am," is one example and "Adieu dear Alderson. Think of me whenever you cannot find anything better to think about" is another.

Correspondence between Mason, Walpole and Alderson was voluminous, containing comments of their scheming on the political issues of the day. Mason's family was staunchly Whig and he spent much of his life in opposition to the government – to the policies of Lord Bute and to those of Lord North during the American war. Alderson, too, was in the thick of it. They were active campaigners in the anti-slavery movement, William Wilberforce, also from Hull, being a personal friend. Mason preached against slavery from the pulpit and in 1777 he baptised a young American black man, one Benjamin Moor, in York Minster, knowing full well that the archbishop would disapprove.

From rectory garden to great estate, Christopher played a part in laying out the gardens of Nuneham Courtenay in Oxfordshire. His precise contribution is unclear but it would have been Mason who brought him in and no one would have been better placed to appreciate the magic in his horticultural fingers.

The first Earl Harcourt chose the site at Nuneham for its superior landscaping qualities with views above the Thames looking towards the spires of Oxford. He had a villa built in 1757 which was later extended into a neo-classical Palladian "seat" at the insistence of his wife. Harcourt was a consummate courtier, holding high office under George II. He was variously Ambassador to Paris, Lord Lieutenant of Ireland and Governor to the Prince of Wales, later George III. In 1760 he travelled to Mecklenburg to escort Princess Charlotte to England to be Queen. Rather carelessly, Harcourt came to a sticky end, best described by Walpole: "The dinner bell had rung, the Earl did not appear, and was found standing on his head in a well, dead!" He had been trying to rescue his pet dog at Nuneham Courtenay. The dog survived to tell the tale.

The second Earl was a republican, though he grew out of it. He was a friend and disciple of Rousseau, and he it was who set about laying out the Nuneham gardens. The park was landscaped by Capability Brown but Harcourt determined that the gardens would be done without professional help and called upon his friend Mason, who designed the famous flower garden on the site of the old village cemetery.

Mason's flower garden embodied the theories he put forward in *The*

Christopher Alderson by Joseph Wright Derby.

English Garden in 1772 and is his only surviving landscape memorial. The architectural focus was the temple of Flora. He mingled wild and garden flowers in aggressively irregular beds, twined jasmine and woodbine round the trees, laced the winding path with Rousseau's favourite flower, the periwinkle, and sprinkled bird seed to entice the linnets and ring doves.

The garden is alongside the north eastern front of the house and was the earliest informal flower garden in the country. Walpole considered it "a quintessential of nosegays." Nuneham has been described as a wonderful example of a garden that is not only a monument to the personalities of its creators, but also a microcosm of them.

The house is now in the possession of the World Spiritual University. Much of the gardens have been lost but a determined attempt is being made to restore at least part of them, and the grotto survives.

Princess Charlotte of Mecklenburg-Strelitz arrived in England at the age of eighteen to become Queen to George III, having first been carefully vetted to ensure that she had no interest in politics whatsoever and had little or no intellectual tastes.

The Queen was to produce fifteen children for the King but beyond the bedroom and the nursery she needed an outlet for her energies and it was to botany that she turned, for intellectual tastes the Queen certainly had. In 1772, on the death of his mother, Princess Augusta, the King inherited Kew and this gave his young Queen the perfect opportunity to develop what became an all-consuming interest. The great botanist, Sir Joseph Banks, became a close friend and the Earl of Bute, the King's chief minister, encouraged Charlotte in her passion for horticulture.

The Queen became an exemplary botanist in her own right and had a considerable influence throughout the great estates of England. She also became an accomplished illustrator, and taught her daughters likewise, recording virtually every specimen of plant life at Kew with considerable skill. She was one of the first to make pressings of flowers. Her interest in botany was to help her through the difficult times that lay ahead as the King's porphyria took hold, and his raves and ravages made life unbearable in the royal household.

In 1792 George III bought Frogmore House alongside Windsor Castle. This was to be the perfect escape from his excesses for the Queen and it was at Frogmore that Charlotte's botanical dreams were fully realised.

Christopher Alderson had assisted in laying out the gardens of Hornby Castle, the seat of the Earls of Holderness. His friend and champion, Mary Darcy, widow of the 4th and last Earl, was a lady of the bedchamber and she introduced Alderson to the Queen.

Queen Charlotte dated the creation of "my little Paradise" from 7 February 1791 when she began her planting with Christopher Alderson, who had undertaken "to render this unpretty thing pretty." The Queen thought Alderson "a man of great natural taste but not of the world." Mason had expressed the philosophical aspect of landscape gardening in four books of poetry published between 1772 and 1782, and it was on these that Alderson modelled his talents. In tandem with her Vice-Chamberlain, Major William Price, Christopher converted a flat site into "a pleasing diversity of mounts, glades, serpentine walks, and canals with bridges and other erections" wrote the enthusiastic Queen.

The name Frogmore is a literal one, pointing to a murky past, and the joint achievement of Price and Alderson was an evocation of landscape gardening amid the fells and dales of Yorkshire. They never got rid of the frogs, whose ancestral haunt it was and still is, but from the old prim parterres and outlying wilds they created a unique and historic garden, varied by the "erections" indispensable to contemporary taste. A century later another Queen was to find Frogmore the perfect resting place for the Mausoleum of her consort prince who died all too young.

Closer to home Christopher was involved in a number of gardens in Derbyshire, among them Norton Hall, Romiley Hall, Renishaw (near Eckington) and The Pastures.

The Sitwells became involved with Renishaw when the first George

Sitwell acquired the land in 1625 and had the Manor House built that forms the centre of the present day Hall. The gardens were reworked and terraced and in the 18th century Renishaw was described as "the most beautiful place in Derbyshire" and in 1776 in Universal Magazine as "a good example of the elder style." Not for much longer, however.

In 1797 the landscapists got to work reducing the garden about the Hall to a field in the style triumphed by Lancelot 'Capability Brown', wrote Sir George Sitwell in his unpublished work *The History of an Old Garden*. He went on to say "At Renishaw the instigator of the barbarous work may have been the rector Mr Alderson… he unfortunately survived until 1818." Sir George is correct in identifying the Rector of Aston as Mr Alderson, though it was in 1814 when he died. Extensions to the Hall in the Regency period were disastrous for the garden with the lime avenue on the top lawn the only garden feature surviving the fashion for bringing "nature right up to the house." This was the landscape that Sir George Sitwell inherited and would have remained but for his own horticultural enlightenment. Between the years 1886-1889 Sir George set out to recreate a garden to suit the house, based largely on what had pertained before Brown and Alderson got to work. And that is what the visitor to Renishaw sees today.

The Pastures is located on the south side of Rykneld Street in Littleover, near Derby. It was built as a villa in 1790 and was substantially extended in 1806 for John Peel, who may have been a cousin of Christopher's. The Peels have a number of walk-on parts in the annals of the Alderson family. John was the seventh son of Robert Peel, a cotton magnate from Blackburn, whose eldest son was created a baronet, and who in turn became the father of the prime minister of the same name. Christopher's grandson, also Christopher, and son of Jonathan and Anna Maria Hodgson, married Peel's granddaughter, Georgiana, at Barlborough.

Today, most of the estate of The Pastures has been built upon though some of Christopher's fine park remains, particularly the lake which has lost little of its charm. A local angler told the author that it was good for fishing. The Pastures was the Rykneld Hospital until 1980 and is now the home of Derby Independent Grammar School.

The Mason/Walpole correspondence gives a good insight into Alderson's lifestyle and his involvement in the affairs of the day. He regularly delivered Mason's letters and messages to Walpole at Strawberry Hill.

Frogmore

Writing to Mason after a visit to Aston in August 1772, Walpole states: "My journey was as agreeable as it could be after leaving so pleasant a place and such good company and was attended by no accident except from an escape from being drowned in a torrent of whores and apprentices at Barnet races." Walpole was unimpressed by Clumber and Thoresby, found Strawberry "parched to the bone" on his return, yet his "so charming bed chamber finished so now have lost all envy of Castle Howard." Walpole complained that "the tomb [in Yorkshire] of William of Hatfield, son of Queen Philippa [wife of Edward III] is tossed about without a yard of earth it can call its own." But he still managed to "Send my compliments to Mr Alderson."

In the following year there was heated correspondence about the merits of an oration by Sir Thomas Whyat, admired by Walpole because "...his soul was vigorous, his genius manly and he was an able statesman." Mason retorted "You know that neither I nor my curate [Alderson] perfectly relished Sir Tomas Wyat's [Walpole's spelling] eloquence and yet my curate and I are neither of us dupes of fashion, but speak what we think in all simplicity .... to follow our plain Yorkshire taste." Walpole found this "inconceivable" saying "It is the finest piece that has been composed since the Romans died." To which Mason retorted "Sir

Thomas's life will be read with pleasure by people that cannot wade through his speech, amongst whom (pardon my anti-antiquarian infirmity) is your humble servant, though I had the hippocricy to scold my curate for owning the same defect of taste." A final dig from Mason: "This [letter] comes by my un-antiquarian curate."

In 1775 Mason expressed concern to Walpole that Lord Holderness had disposed of his Aston estates in small parcels "which will occasion so much difficulty in regulating my tithes" adding that the matter will "be all settled by my curate Mr Alderson, on whose judgement and honesty I can fully depend upon," but that he [Mason] "must appear to do it myself to prevent any odium that might fall upon him [Alderson] from the parish."

In 1783 we find "My friend Mr Alderson brings you with this the copies you requested of Gray's head. He comes as a negotiator between poor Lady Holderness and her quondam son-in-law, [presumably Mad Jack Byron] who by taking advantage of a lawyer's blunder in Lord Holderness's will is likely to distress her exceedingly and I shall not wonder if the house, pictures, etc. in Hertford Street follows Sion Hill" [which Lady Holderness had apparently lost, although Lord Holderness left it to her as a life interest]. "Tis a sad business and I pity her extremely."

Lady Holderness applied to General Conway, Commander in Chief of the Army, about an ensigncy for a young Alderson relative. Mason, writing to Walpole in support, says "The commission wanted is for any place or service, and not to make a parading officer in the park. The young man is at present rather a burden on his relation ... and ... has a family of his own."

Walpole discovered that Conway had "Put him on the list" but "that was before the conclusion of the war, when he thought it would rain ensigncies, and that he is now left with above an hundred engagements, and that the new plan of seconding two companies [I don't understand military Hebrew] with their officers on all the corps will increase his difficulty of performing them." Walpole, nevertheless, asked Mason "to desire that Mr Alderson call on me in town on Friday; and this I send to London, by a gentleman who dines with me, to Lord Harcourt, who will deliver it to you on the Birthday [the King's on 4 June]." On 6 June Walpole confirmed "I have seen Mr Alderson and told him what General Conway says, to whom I have spoken again."

Later "Re: your letter of the 19th Mr Alderson left it at my door just as I was getting into my chaise to come hither, and did not send up word that he was there, or I should certainly have desired to see him. However, I wrote a line immediately to General Conway" .... and .... "I expect to hear tomorrow before he goes away."

The regiments were soon to be broken because of the peace and no Alderson appears in the Army Lists for the next ten years. This was probably as well from Walpole's point of view, as we soon find him telling Mason "cruel to have boys by favour put over old officers." Two months earlier he had asked Conway to resist helping his nephew.

The poet Thomas Gray travelled widely throughout Britain in search of picturesque scenery and ancient monuments and Christopher Alderson transcribed a large part of his tour of the Lake District and Yorkshire in 1769 for the *Memoirs of Gray.*

In 1774 Mason was waiting to hear from "my curate Mr Alderson who is now at Syon Hill and who will soon give me an account not only of his Lordship's present state of health, but his intended motions." In the same year from Nuneham, Mason wrote "I am obliged to go to town before I can visit Strawberry Hill to settle matters with Lord Holderness in connection with his approaching presentation to the Rectory of Langton-upon-Swale." Alderson was the Rector of Langton, in the North Riding, from 1768-77 so perhaps this refers to a curate.

In 1778 Mason tells us "I had one thought of passing through town but the absence of my curate [Alderson], I believe, will prevent me, for he is setting off with Lord H's corpse for Hornby and is to return to town to settle some affairs relative to the lease of Sion Hill with the Duke of Northumberland." Lord Holderness was buried at Hornby on 1 June 1778, Mason officiating at the funeral.

On a more politic note, Mason and Alderson were worried at the Gordon riots, Protestant opposition to the repeal of anti-Catholic laws. Things got completely out of hand in 1779 and Mason tells Walpole of "Bringing this large county [Yorkshire] together to consider the critical state of landed property. Matters are now growing so near a crisis that despotism or a struggle against it, and a warm one too, is to be expected. Tame submission will indeed spare present bloodshed - but - you can make the inference without my assistance. If the person who brings this should chance to meet with you at home he will tell you all I know of myself, and of my motions, nor is he ignorant of the contents for I know he may be trusted" and "My curate will know how to forward all letters to me by the very same post that brings them."

On 31 March 1797 Mason injured his leg whilst entering his carriage. The wound became inflamed over the weekend and Alderson reported "Mr Mason was suddenly seized by a violent shivering fit and never spoke afterwards... It seemed as if his whole frame had given way at once; for the malady was so rapid that he died the day following." Christopher was his executor and had a memorial erected to him in All Saints Church, Aston. He is also believed to have been instrumental in having Mason remembered in Poets' Corner at Westminster Abbey.

In 1780 arms were granted to Christopher, the blazon of arms being:

Arms: Per pale, 1st, azure a chevron engrailed ermine between three suns in splendor, a label of three points.

Crest: Behind a mount vert thereon a branch of alder the sun rising proper.

It is said that the punning crest of the alder tree and the sun was suggested by Queen Charlotte but the real surprise is that the grant included "...the other posterity of his father according to the laws of arms." Thus Jonathan Alderson of High Ewebank was included. When confirming this in 1997, Robert Noel, Bluemantle Pursuivant at the College of Arms, emphasised his approval by stating that he was "delighted to hear that Jonathan had so many sons who in turn have been progenitive." In further conversation he confirmed that records of the application no longer exist but suggested that a sufficiently indulgent herald, possibly with a prompt from Christopher, was persuaded to include his father in the grant. Hence Jonathan's other sons and their descendants would benefit as time passed.

Christopher was paid £40 per annum as Mason's curate and for some of his time at least he took lodgings, one presumes to a goodly standard, in Aston village. His duties were far from merely ecclesiastical for he was very much Mason's right hand man on matters domestic, his representative when the rector was away, which was often, and his confidante when he was at home with whom he shared every confidence and sought second opinions on the great issues of the day.

We are left with some interesting domestic snippets of life at Aston. Mason encouraged Christopher to "...go on with your Chemical processes" ...for he was not aware that "Gum Dragon would dissolve in spirit of wine." He suggested that clear spirit of turpentine might do better to darken the colours. When Mason was to spend the winter in London he asked Christopher to send him a couple of pigs and a small basket of pears by the Doncaster Fly. Instructions were given regarding the bee hives and Mason asks Christopher to save for him "two of Kitty's puppys and those the smallest will be enough for me." And Christopher is given instructions regarding a maid: "Send her back to her relations for the winter...she is too dressy a Lady for my service."

Writing from St James's Palace in 1769 Mason tells Christopher that "I saw your Qualifications for the Chaplaincy signed yesterday" and then advises that Dr Gisbourn recommends that "...you should go on with Magnesium, if he does

The Alderson Coat of Arms

not disapprove my camomile prescription." Mason presumes Christopher's illness to be brought on by overwork and promises to bring some of the best Magnesium with him but instructs him "...in the mean time to take what Sheffield produces."

From Curzon Street Mason tells Christopher not to want for moneys expended on his behalf and expresses the hope that he has distributed corn to the poorer part of his parishioners "in such proportions as you think propper."

Christopher was a magistrate on the Sheffield bench. Lecturing a sturdy vagabond on one occasion before sentencing him, he told him:

"The Almighty's given you health and strength, 'stead of which you go about stealing ducks."

Christopher Alderson was painted by Joseph Wright of Derby in 1794, one of Wright's last portraits. The author has in his possession Christopher's French Bible, New Testament only. It is not known to what degree Christopher travelled but during his mature years the Napoleonic wars were in full swing.

Christopher died at Eckington on 27 March 1814 aged 76 years. *Gentleman's Magazine* tells us that he suffered for ten years from the distressing complaint of tic doulouvent, painful spasms of the facial muscles. He is buried at Aston.

Christopher and Elizabeth Alderson had three sons and two daughters, Jonathan, William, Christopher, Elizabeth and Mary.

6

Rev. Jonty Alderson
and the Hodgsons

Jonathan Alderson, the eldest son of Christopher and Elizabeth Alderson, née Ball, was baptised at Aston on 6 August 1769. Unlike his father, Jonty was born into wealth, reaping the benefits of his father's advancements. Not for him the windswept moors except, perhaps, as a landowner of considerable acreage upon which he might have cast an occasional disdainful eye.

It followed that Jonty's route to Cambridge was more conventional than his father's. He was admitted as a pensioner at Pembroke on 28 May 1788 when he was eighteen years old. He obtained his BA in 1792, his MA in 1795 and the same year became Rector of Langton-upon-Swale.

Rev. Jonathan Alderson

Jonathan was a tall, good looking man, judging by Moore's portrait of 1822, when he would have been 53 years old. He had an intelligent face, a high forehead and delicate features.

On 7 June 1798 Jonty was married by licence in Sheffield Cathedral to Anna Maria Hodgson, the only daughter of the Rev Rowland Hodgson, Rector of Rawmarsh. Thus one wealthy Yorkshire clergyman had ensured that his eldest son married the daughter of another, for

Rawmarsh, three miles north of Rotherham, was again a well endowed parish.

Hodgson was Rector of Rawmarsh from 1766 to 1796, which is confirmed by a memorial plaque in the church which states "Sacred to the memory of Rev. Rowland Hodgson, Thirty years Rector of this parish who died March 26th 1796 aged 78 and Mary his wife who died February 6th 1782 aged 50." The burial register records him as "the worthy Rector of this parish" and Mary as " daughter of John Parker Esq., of Woodthorpe." There is an area of Sheffield called Woodthorpe which might have been the Parkers' original home. They are buried in the churchyard, though the location is unknown.

Anna Maria Hodgson

The original church at Rawmarsh dates from the mid 12th century and was little changed until Rowland decided to bring it into the modern world. In 1780 he initiated an ambitious project to add a north aisle. He had to obtain a faculty from the Archbishop of York empowering him to enlarge the church by taking down the north wall and extending into the churchyard by ten feet. This enabled him to erect a gallery, add new seats and build a vestry. Unfortunately, in demolishing the north wall, several ancient monuments outside the church were destroyed or damaged, including a large alabaster stone slab which disappeared, part of the grave of Dame Troth Mallory, a great benefactor in her day. It was subsequently sold to a Swinton potter for a guinea.

Whatever "improvements" Hodgson might have rendered to Rawmarsh Church were as nothing compared to its virtual demolition in 1837 in order to facilitate yet another enlargement. Hodgson's construction was mostly flattened but thanks must be accorded to the great and the good of Rawmarsh, for at least they retained the Norman tower.

The benefice of Rawmarsh was a wealthy one in Hodgson's day. His name appears on a list, published in 1780, of householders liable to pay tax on male servants. Most of the wealth derived from the church lands which increased substantially in value due to the discovery of rich seams of coal. The Rectors of Rawmarsh were large landowners during Hodgson's time and when the commons were enclosed in 1784, the award showed that he owned 174 acres 3 roods and 38 perches. His income from tithes, commuted to rents, was over £38 per annum, and in all likelihood there were further tithes from other lands.

Prior to Hodgson's time, Rectors of Rawmarsh did not have curates but Rowland had at least two. By the late 18th century the population was rising rapidly as the mineral wealth of the parish was further exploited. In the 19th century the southern part of the parish, that adjoining Rotherham, became the newly created parish of Christ Church, Parkgate, with a large population engaged in steel and chemicals production.

The Rectory in which Hodgson lived still stands, though only just. It was built in 1752 with fifteen rooms, but the Victorians extended it, making it far too large for a 20th century rector. The diocese disposed of it in the early 1980s and had a smaller rectory, and also a nursing home, built in the garden. The old rectory has been badly vandalised and is now in a dangerous state; indeed, despite being a listed building it is just a matter of time before the whole thing is pulled down, or otherwise comes

Rawmarch Church today

41

tumbling down of its own accord.

Anna Maria's mother, Mary Hodgson, would have been 39 years old in 1771 when her daughter was born (and Rowland in his 50s) and 41 when her only other child, also Rowland, was born in 1773. Anna Maria's portrait shows a firmness of mouth and focussed eyes suggesting a quiet determination, softened by hair in ringlets resting on her shoulders.

In 1804 Jonty Alderson became vicar of Hornby in North Yorkshire, succeeding his younger brother William, who had held the living since 1800. Jonathan was vicar until 1829 and was then succeeded by his eldest son George. Thus three Aldersons of two generations were the incumbents at Hornby for no less than 80 years.

Hornby is the quintessential English village, set in lush rolling hills south of Richmond. St Mary's is a beautiful church with a long history dating back to the 11th century. Much of the tower is Saxon and the church is overshadowed by the walls of the castle which was built by the St Quentins shortly after the Conquest. Over the centuries, and via marriage, the Quentins became the Conyers-Darceys and were created the Earls of Holderness in 1682 and held the castle and estate for many years. The 4th Earl died in 1778 and, having outlived his sons, his estates passed to his daughter, Amelia, (the mother of Augusta Byron) who had earlier married the Marquis of Carmarthen who later become the 5th Duke of Leeds. The castle then became the northern seat of the dukes.

The last duke hated Hornby and demolished much of it, selling the stones to a rich American. He disposed of the remainder of the estate in 1929. The castle nevertheless remains a fine sight to this day, particularly as one approaches Hornby from the north. It has for some years been in the possession of Major General Clutterbuck.

The Vicarage in Jonathan's time is believed to have been called North Field House, later renamed Winterfield House, a pretty house which still exists, just north of the church, and it is here that many of his children were born. Anna Maria was to bear Jonathan eight children, three boys and five girls viz: George born in 1799, Christopher in 1803, Augusta Mary in 1806, Jonathan in 1809, Sarah in 1812 and Elizabeth, Charlotte Augusta and Anna Maria. Many of them lived to a good age, the last surviving being Anna Maria who died in 1908.

In 1824 the Vicarage was abandoned for a much grander edifice, which presumably was built under Jonathan's tutelage.

In 1812 Jonathan was presented to the living of Harthill by the Duke of

Hornby Vicarage

Leeds, and was Rector there until his death. Harthill is the southernmost village in Yorkshire, located just four miles from both Aston and Eckington. Florence Sitwell of the Renishaw family, noted in her diary "...attending a pretty fete in the Garden at Barlborough, under the great oak, [were] four young Miss Aldersons, daughters of the Rev. Jonathan Alderson of Harthill, in apple-green silk dresses, with large white chip hats wreathed round with pink roses. (I never saw any of these last-mentioned ladies again till I met the two survivors at Scarborough exactly fifty years after!)."

The seat of the Duke of Leads was nearby Kiveton Hall, since demolished. The family's rise to prosperity began with one Edward Osborn, a poor boy who went to London to seek his fortune. There he prospered, became Lord Mayor of London, and was knighted, his descendants eventually being raised to the dukedom.

Anna Maria's mother, Mary Hodgson (née Parker), was the younger of John Parker's two daughters and in 1813 Mary's sister, Sarah, died, followed by her husband, George Woodhead, two months later. The Woodheads were childless and George left almost the whole of his considerable property to his "favourite niece and nephew" to the indignation of his cousin Gertrude's children. The estate included Highfield in Sheffield, which was let to tenants of "suitable respectability." Among these, from 1843, was James Wilson, grandson of the "famous" John Wilson of Broomhead, who in 1825 had married Jonathan and Anna Maria's daughter, Elizabeth, of whom more anon.

Highfield Terrace remained within the family until 1879 when it was sold at auction for £1,500 in order to clear up some lawsuit about the shares of different members of the family. It must have been well built for it was still there in the mid 1970s, and in all probability is to this day. Favourite nephew Jonty, however is not forgotten, for adjoining the terrace are Alderson Road and Alderson Place, the latter running into Bramall Lane, the home of Sheffield United Football Club and, for more than 100 years until 1973, of Yorkshire County Cricket Club.

Both Anna Maria and Jonathan died in 1848, Anna on New Year's day and Jonathan of diabetes on 9 September. They are buried in a splendid tomb in Harthill Churchyard. A memorial plaque in the church tells us that Jonathan was "The beloved pastor of this parish for 36 years" and that "his last illness was accompanied by the most acute bodily pain and suffering and was borne by him with such patience and resignation as the principles of the Gospel of Jesus Christ alone can give." The inscription tells us he was "Universally respected and esteemed and the poor especially have lost in him a most liberal and sympathising friend."

~ ~ ~ ~ ~ ~ ~ ~ ~ ~ ~ ~ ~ ~

Jonathan's brother, William, graduated from Pembroke College, Cambridge in 1795 and was awarded his MA in 1804. Following his four years at Hornby he was appointed perpetual curate at Tissington in Derbyshire by the patron, Sir Henry Fitzherbert, who became a lifelong friend. William became Rector of Aston in 1811 in succession to his father, the Rev. Christopher Alderson. In 1813 he married Harriet, eldest daughter of Joseph Walker, an ironmaster of Eastwood near Rotherham and of Aston, and sister to Sir Edward Samuel Walker of Mansfield. William and Harriet had no children.

William was Rector of Aston for 40 years and *Gentleman's Magazine* tells us that he was a diligent and caring minister, in particular to the poor of the parish whom he employed whenever possible. He gave liberal assistance to the distressed, superintended children's education and was a regular visitor to the sick. We are also told that he bequeathed Mason's favourite chair to Rev. John Mitford, who subsequently gave it to Tennyson, the Poet Laureate.

Like his brother and father he acquired considerable wealth, owning estates jointly with, amongst others, William Pitt, (Lord Amherst), the Earl of Chichester and George Lane Fox of Bramham Park. William was also an executor to the Duke of Leeds.

William died in 1852 and is buried at Aston in a vault on the south side of the church, near the chancel door, close to where Mason lies. His cousin, Charles Macro Wilson, a Sheffield solicitor who acted as administrator of the estate, expressed satisfaction that William had willed a legacy of £100 to the West Riding Charity for the Relief of Widows of Clergymen.

Harriet outlived William by 29 years and had a sense of adventure, for in 1818 she set off on an ambitious drive from Aston to North Wales and Anglesey, a return journey, with detours, of 581 miles. She was accompanied by Lady Fitzherbert and recorded her impressions in an observant and witty diary. The party travelled in two carriages, a phaeton and a post chaise for the servants - a necessity rather then a luxury in the early 19th century.

Harriet commences her diary by describing the drive across the Pennines to Middleton, "a large village singularly scattered upon the side of a rock." She found Middleton Dale extremely romantic "huge masses of stone having been united by art but Chapel-en-le-Frith a miserable place, though convenient to change the horses." They passed through Macclesfield and Knutsford to Chester, where they stayed for three days, and found the accommodation good but the charges high. They heard that two Stockport weavers had been imprisoned for two years for rioting, they visited the lead works and they went to Eaton, the "magnificent seat of Lord Grosvenor." Then into Wales.

What was defective in accommodation at the White Horse Inn at Holywell was amply rewarded by the civility of the landlady. They passed Sunday there, and heard a good sermon from the vicar. His text was delivered in Welsh, the rest of his discourse in English. The road from St Asaph through the Vale of Clwyd was interspersed with many gentlemen's seats, and "Conway's majestic towers burst unexpectedly upon us," though the best accommodation they could find was "a small and dirty inn and the charges very high." The road to Bangor was "sublime grandeur."

Our intrepid travellers were surprised at the lack of bathing machines at Beaumaris, they discovered that China Rock supplies much of itself to the Staffordshire potteries, they met the clergyman at Capel Curig who was also the landlord, (though he delegated responsibilities for this to his wife), and they found Harlech a wretched town. "The inn was no better than a pot house and the inhabitants in a state of greatest poverty, the elections for Merionethshire being held in a house without a roof."

Caernarfon Castle was grand and elegant and their visit to Plas Newydd in Anglesey was enjoyed, though the memorial to the lost leg of Waterloo was considered to be in bad taste. Finally to Snowdon, majestically presenting itself, "one of the finest scenes I had ever viewed and filled my mind with awe and admiration." The gentlemen made the ascent, a walk of nine miles, which took ten hours. Harriet did not include a list of her travelling companions and there is no mention of William in her diary. The likelihood is that he stayed at home to look after his flock.

The third son of Christopher and Elizabeth Alderson, also Christopher, was in a different mould to his two brothers. He lived variously at Aston, London and Caernarfon (did Harriet visit her brother-in-law, one wonders?) and is said to have spoken Welsh fluently. He may have been at one time clerk to the Constable of Caernarfon Castle, the constable usually being the Prince of Wales.

Any story of Christopher must be taken with a generous grain of salt. He was always short of money and asking other members of the family for loans. He is said to have been put into the Fleet Prison for embezzlement from the Duke of Leeds, eventually being bailed out by his wife's family. In 1835, however, he was Chairman of the Carnarvon Magistrates! In that capacity Christopher received a letter from prisoner Owen Owens from the goal requesting a pair of shoes, "for my shoes was good when first came heare" wrote prisoner Owen Owens, "but during the space of nine Weeks which I have been confined here …entirely done and having know (now) to work on the treadmill I am in great pain as the(y) will not stay on me feet and being unable to get a pair my self I therefor appeal to ye as the county magistrates."

In 1809, writing from Aston to his friend Pease, (the railway Pease one wonders?) Christopher apologised for missing him in Hull but he had "suddenly been called to Beverley to give evidence against a man who had been talking seditiously in front of his men and which had been largely responsible for the mutiny amongst them." He invited Pease to visit Aston where "There was fishing and shooting, a good library and the Iron Works at Rotherham to see." If he came by coach a horse would be provided.

Christopher was in London for a spell as a clerk in Mr Bradley's bro-ker's office, his fees having been paid by his sister. He liked Mr Bradley, who had started the business five years earlier and had made a handsome fortune. He commented that three men had been hanged, one for sodomy, one for rape and the third for assisting the offence, punishments that he considered were not severe enough.

He had been greatly impressed by the King's (George II) Jubilee "The affection with which the King was held was manifest." He had seen the procession of the Lord Mayor to address the King who "...looked like a mountebank and the coach, drawn by six white horses, looked like a stage coach."

Christopher's first wife died and is buried at Caernarfon. He married secondly Margaret Peat Frith. In 1819 Christopher Alderson wrote from the south Yorkshire village of Wales reporting that his two brothers lived nearby, Jonathan as Rector of Harthill who had eight children, and William as Rector of Aston who had none and that he "had two stout boys." They were Alfred and Dennis. Dennis died at Cambridge in 1838, aged 24 years. Alfred appears to have been a bit of a wag. He was articled to Robert Williams, a Caernarfon solicitor, between 1835 and 1838. He married Frances Elizabeth Wasteneys and they had five chil-dren.

Alfred Alderson was sent to London in 1839 to train in the law. Taking a walk one day he noticed a crowd outside St James's Palace. He ascer-tained that the Queen was about to come out, and later penned this fan-ciful, not to say extraordinary, account of what happened next:

I put my hands into my pockets to take care of what was in them and watched Her Majesty's arrival. A body of Horse Guards was waiting for her at the door and just before she came out their beautiful band of Guards marched past playing a beautiful thing, followed by the Guards and when about half had passed the gates they were commanded to halt and divide into two companies. Then the garden gates were opened by two porters covered over with gold. Then a carriage made its appearance in which were three pages splendidly dressed and a Lord in Waiting, then a second carriage with Ladies in it drawn by two horses and driven by one coachman and pushed along by two footmen. Next came a carriage drawn by two horses driven by one coachman and four footmen each carrying a cane with an immense gold head with which they kill all the flies that fly in the direction of the windows, knobble the heads of the people as they pass to put them in mind that the next carriage contains royalty and in this carriage sat our Gracious Queen who moved of course to me because I took off my hat, about the only one who did. She smiled very graciously at me and invited me to dine with her. I said I was engaged, otherwise should have been most happy. Now in fact I was not engaged but having made myself sure that Lord Melbourne would be there I would not disgrace myself by sitting at table with such a man. The Queen looked very well but was not cheered at all as she is very unpopular.

The youthful Queen had committed a number of indiscretions in the first years of her reign, before the arrival of the guiding hand of Albert.

During his stay in London Alfred visited a flea circus which excited him somewhat. He went to church at St Clement's in the Strand and strongly approved of the sermon preached by Mr McNeil in support of the Protestant Association. Clearly he was not a Liberal for he cheered lustily when, in May 1839, Lord Melbourne was forced to resign.

Alfred's five children were born at Eckington but only one had issue. His eldest son, also Alfred, died young. Sisters Ann and Sarah both remained spinsters and lived to be 74 and 78 years old respectively. They lived much of their lives in Chesterfield before moving to a beautiful Georgian house opposite the church in Barlborough. His youngest son, Christopher, a solicitor, was killed hunting with Lord Galway's Hounds in 1903 and thus the Alderson name in this line died out with him. He is buried at Killamarsh.

Alfred's third daughter, Frances Margaret Alderson, married Charles Howes-Smith in 1873. They had a son, Thomas Alfred Howes-Smith, who in 1904 married Florence Mary Hunter, the daughter of a scythe and sickle manufacturer. They in turn were the parents of Florence Mary Margaret Howes-Smith, born in 1905, and Christopher Alderson Howes-Smith, born the following year. Margaret was intelligent and unflappable and was secretary to the Magistrates Court for many years until retiring at 60. She then worked part time until well into her 70s, for the Sitwells of Renishaw, in support of the Estate Treasurer. She lived at Barlborough in north Derbyshire, close to Eckington, and was loyal to the church which had played so large a part in her family's history. She died aged 94 in 2000, proud to have made it into the new millennium.

Christopher Alderson Howes-Smith was my Godfather and it is to him that I am indebted for so much of the Alderson story. I much enjoyed being shown round the "Alderson" parishes that straddle the Yorkshire/Derbyshire boundary; Harthill, Aston, Eckington, Barlborough, Wales and Killamarsh.

Christopher Alderson Howes-Smith was a countryman through and through, hunting and shooting but not fishing which he found too tame. He was born at Killamarsh in north Derbyshire. He was a tall upright man with an impish sense of humour. Whilst learning farming in Northamptonshire he claimed Lady Elizabeth Bowes Lyon as his dancing partner and years later would boast that he hunted with the Prince of Wales (Prince Charles). He joined the RAF at the outbreak of war and in 1940 married Freda Mary Holmes. Their honeymoon in Clumber Park was disrupted somewhat as they were blown out of bed by a bomb on their wedding night and next morning Christopher's leave was abruptly cancelled. They had one daughter, Janet Mary who was born in 1942. In 1985 she married Robert John Romilly Salt and they live at Rhyl in North Wales.

7

Jonathan Alderson
Soldier and Farmer

Jonathan Alderson, my two greats grandfather, was the third son and the fourth of the eight children of Rev. Jonty Alderson and Anna Maria, née Hodgson. He was born on 5 February 1809 at Hornby, in the North Riding of Yorkshire, where his father was vicar. This was a critical time in the country's history for the Peninsular war was raging and as a six year old boy, he would have been excited by the victory at Waterloo. Perhaps this is what drew him towards the army, for in 1828, when he was nineteen years old, he joined the 43rd Regiment of Foot, the Monmouthshires.

The 43rd of Foot was raised in 1741 as one of Sir John Moore's original light infantry regiments. Jonathan had no link with the Welsh border county which might explain why this first attempt by the army to call upon regional loyalties was not a success. In 1881 the regiment became the 1st Battalion the Oxfordshire Light Infantry and in 1908 it was absorbed into the Oxfordshire and Buckinghamshire Light Infantry. Finally, in 1966, it became part of the Royal Green Jackets.

Jonathan joined the 43rd at Gibraltar as an ensign on 9 September 1828. He was promoted to Lieutenant on 6 April 1831 and left the army in 1834. Thus his army career was sandwiched between Waterloo and the Crimea and no great battles or campaigns were fought.

Jonathan had only been with the regiment a week, however, when he had his first escape, for on 17 September the soldiers were moved out of barracks and placed under canvas because a "mortal epidemic" had broken out in the garrison. Cholera one suspects. Losses included two sergeants, one bugler and 86 rank and file, amongst them many of the finest and most athletic soldiers in the corps. Not until 10 January 1829 did the regiment return to barracks, the scourge having at last subsided.

In December 1830 serious disturbances broke out at home, most likely associated with the Reform Bill. The Admiral's flag-ship, the *Windsor Castle,* was commandeered on its way home from Malta and the whole of the 43rd, with little or no preparation - men, women, children and baggage - were hustled on board. They quit Gibraltar the same night, 17 December 1830. Shortly after setting sail, whilst passing through the Strait of Gibraltar, the batteries at Tarifa opened up, one shot flying over the poop and another striking the ship just under the quarter-galley. Guns were ordered to be manned but the current carried the *Windsor Castle* out of range before battle could be joined. It later transpired that the *Windsor Castle* had drifted closer to the coast than she should have and Jack Spaniard was waiting. This apart, the regimental archives tell us that it was an uneventful voyage to Portsmouth, "with much good humoured banter between the brave tars and their red-coated passengers."

The regiment disembarked at Portsmouth on 2 January and marched to Winchester Barracks

Jonathan Alderson of the 43rd.

where, by express command, it was detained until the arrival of the Duke of Wellington, who had travelled down from London to inspect his old tried and favourite corps. The regiment travelled up to Manchester in

February, it then consisting of three field-officers, ten captains, ten lieutenants, ten ensigns, six staff, 42 sergeants, 36 corporals, fourteen buglers, and 653 privates. The head-quarters was set up at Wigan in support of the civil power while four companies marched to Newcastle-under-Lyme "in consequence of insurrectionary ebullitions in the Potteries."

In January 1832 the regiment moved to Dublin to enforce peace in Ireland, later moving head-quarters to Kilkenny with detachments located throughout Ireland. In August 1834 the whole regiment moved to Cork and it was here that Jonathan left the army.

In 1838 at Worksop, Jonathan was commissioned into the Nottinghamshire Yeomanry, the Sherwood Rangers, rather like today's Territorial Army.

At least two likenesses of Jonathan exist, a water colour in the possession of the family and a portrait in oils in the head quarters of the Royal Green Jackets Regiment at Winchester. This latter is a copy painted by H. M. Haymore of Broadstairs, based on an original by Nicholas Condy which was painted at Devonport in 1829. The two are almost identical, the main difference being that the Royal Green Jackets version shows a background of the regiment in action against the French.

Condy has used licence here for the British had not fought the French since Waterloo (as remains the case to this day) but Condy, too, had been in the 43rd and used his experiences from the Peninsular War where the Regiment had been in the thick of it many times. Nicholas Condy is best known for his landscapes, particularly of the Plymouth area, but no doubt was happy to maintain contact with his regiment and pick up some additional commissions. The portrait at Winchester was presented to the museum by Col. Bayley on his retirement in 1927. The whereabouts of the original is unknown.

In both portraits the nineteen year old Jonathan looks very young and innocent. He has small features, a sensitive mouth, clear blue eyes and a hint of wispish light brown hair, more a picture of boyish innocence than of a soldier who was part of a deadly fighting force. But the nation was at peace and no doubt Jonathan served his King and country well.

Jonathan made the most of the sixteen years that were to remain to him. After leaving the army he married, had a child, was widowed, married a second time, sired a further seven children and died in 1850 at the early age of 41.

Presumably Jonathan left the army to get married, for in the same year, on 27 November 1834 when he was 25, he married his cousin Isabella, the daughter of William Newsham (spelling variations) and Elizabeth Alderson, she the daughter of Christopher "Gardener" Alderson and Elizabeth Ball. Seven months later, on 25 June 1835, William Marmaduke Dixwell Alderson was born and three months after that, on 19 September, Isabella died.

On 16 October 1840 Captain Jonathan Alderson married for a second time, to Georgiana Taylor, daughter of William Taylor, gentleman, of Radcliffe-on-Trent. Jonathan's profession is now recorded as clerk. My great grandfather, George Henry William Alderson, was born at Gedling in Nottinghamshire in 1842. His sister Elizabeth Isabella was born in 1843, Frank in 1844, Anna Julia in 1846 (died in 1849), Arthur Christopher in 1847, Montague Strachan in 1848 and finally Julia Anna, known in later life as Aunt Annie Keatinge, in 1850. Her father died the following month. Of Aunt Annie, more later.

During these later years Jonathan lived at Gannow Hill Farm at Killamarsh in Derbyshire, a property probably first brought into the family by his father. Here he settled down to the life of a gentleman farmer. Whatever its origin, the name Gannow was to achieve a special significance in the annals of this Alderson family, for later generations were to give this name to houses large and small in other parts of the country.

Jonathan has left us a notebook in which he records the business of the day which gives an insight into managing life on the farm in the mid 19th century. Entitled "An account of the Number of Sheep Brought into the House at Gannow Hill," the first entry is for 1 January 1846. We learn that "one sheep weight sixty eight pounds at 7 pence a pound: £1.19. 8d No1." On 13 January "one pork pig seven stone at seven shillings a stone £2.9.0d. No1" and on 16 January sheep No.2 brings in £2/0/3d. On 18 April "sheep the sixth" weighs in and on 8 May "my first lamb." Total income for the year amounted to £30/17/2d for mutton and £19/0/0d for pigs.

At the back of the book Jonathan records an incident in rather confusing yet amusing detail. "I commenced mowing June 15th 1846 on a Monday. Bill Hay and Cousons mowed the lawn at Gannow Hill and got the hay stacked on the Friday in the same week. I gave 3/6d per acre for mowing at Gannow and four shillings per acre at Harthill and no drinks. Tom Cousons and Bill Hay both went away on the Saturday without leave. I gave 3/6d at Gannow and no drink without I choose. The reason why they have 3/6d at Gannow is because there are no hedges. The reason why they have four shillings per acre at Harthill is on account of the hedges and no drink. I will never give Hay and Cousons a drop of drink again for mowing."

Jonathan died at Gannow Hill, on 27 March 1850 of hypertrophy of riverticles - several years rupture of aorta according to his death certificate, though "several years" sounds somewhat implausible.

Gannow Hill Farm is remembered by the lane leading up to it from Killamarsh village, now a modern housing development called Gannow Close.

~ ~ ~ ~ ~ ~ ~ ~ ~ ~ ~ ~ ~

The other children of Rev. Jonathan and Anna Maria were a talented and interesting clutch. George was the eldest and was born in 1799. He married Henrietta Kearsley and succeeded his father as Rector of Hornby, a position he held for more than 30 years. He and his wife are buried outside the church door. The Hornby living was in the gift of the Duke of Leeds, whose chaplain he was.

Next came Christopher, who benefited from the advowson giving him the living of Kirkheaton. He went to Magdalen College, Oxford. An elaborate marriage settlement was drawn up prior to his wedding at Barlborough, to Georgiana Peel. It was a jolly affair, the bride and groom departing to the ringing cheers of no less than 600 Sunday School children, after which everyone sat down to an enormous tea, kindly supplied by the rector himself, Christopher Alderson and his new wife.

The next surviving child was Augusta Mary (1806-1887). Augusta was a spinster and like her brother, was born and brought up at Hornby. She became an accomplished penworker. Penworking, sometimes called Chinese painting or Indian ornamental work, was a means of decorating furniture and was popular in the early 19th century. It was largely practised by amateurs between 1815 and 1850. Neo-classical subjects, chinoiseries or flowers were painted in water colours in reserves leaving the light wood showing on black backgrounds. Augusta was an outstandingly talented artist. Her work, which sometimes embraced Harthill Church, still appears from time to time in the antique salons. A pair of cabinets was seen recently at Mallett's of Bond Street, one of which was inscribed "Commenced painting this Cabinet Sept. 24th 1842. Finished May 23rd 1845. Augusta M Alderson."

Jonathan was next in line and he was followed by four sisters: Sarah who married H Parker, Elizabeth, Charlotte Augusta who married a Mr Hoby and Anna Maria.

Elizabeth is the link with cricket. When I was a boy in Yorkshire my father often told me of our "cousin," the great Yorkshire cricketer Rockley Wilson. I would cheerfully brag about this without having a clue as to the authenticity of the link. It was, however, through Elizabeth, who married James Wilson, Clerk to the Cutlers' Company from 1820 to 1845. They had four sons, one of whom, Canon William Reginald Wilson, vicar of Bolsterstone near Sheffield, married Martha Thorp and they in turn had five sons. The fourth and fifth sons were Clement Eustace Macro Wilson, known as CEM (1875-1944) and Evelyn Rockley Wilson (1879-1957). Both played cricket for Cambridge University, both played for Yorkshire and both played for England.

CEM and Rockley Wilson are the only brothers to have scored centuries for Cambridge in Varsity matches, CEM 115 in 1898 and Rockley 118 in 1901.

CEM played in the inaugural and second Test Matches against South Africa in 1898/9 as a member of Lord Hawke's team. They were at Port Elizabeth and Cape Town and both were won. More than 100 years later, the official South African Tour Brochure for the 1999/2000 Millennium Test Series v. England, included a photograph of this first team and a moustachioed CEM is in the centre on the front row, sitting almost on Lord Hawke's boots.

Rockley Wilson was an outstanding coach at Winchester for 40 years and toured to America, the West Indies, Argentina and to Australia in 1920/21. That was a miserable tour as England lost all five test matches (yes, we have heard that before!). Wilson played in just one test match, the fifth at Sydney. He was a record breaker, though not due to his skills with bat or ball but rather as one of the oldest debutantes in the history of test cricket, no less than 41 years and 337 days old, so Wisden tells us. Jack Hobbs was later to write of the consequences to him of being jeered by the crowd for sloppy fielding. Wilson took exception to this and immediately cabled his objections to the British press. Just as quickly these press reports were relayed back to Australia and when Wilson went in to bat next day he was received with savage hooting from the crowd. When he was out for five the cheering of the crowd was loud and prolonged, even the members in the pavilion joining in. At least Wilson's bowling was a respectable 3 for 36.

One of Wilson's pupils at Winchester was Douglas Jardine who was to captain England during the infamous 1932 "bodyline" series. Mike Coward, writing in the *Australian* newspaper during the Melbourne Boxing Day Test Match of 2002, reminded readers that it was Wilson's words, penned prior to the England team's departure, that "Jardine will probably win us back the Ashes but he will also loose us a dominion" that resounded throughout the British Empire for many years thereafter.

The gap between the test match careers of the brothers was 22 years, in all likelihood a record.

Rockley Wilson played for Yorkshire mainly after the end of the Winchester summer term. Between 1919 and 1921 he took no less than 136 wickets. The *Times* obituary described him as possibly the best amateur length slow bowler the game had known and also "a character, a wit and master of the impromptu and hero of countless anecdotes that lovers of the game and the droll tale derive pleasure in repeating."

Anna Maria, the last surviving daughter of the Rev. Jonathan Alderson, had a plaque erected in Harthill Church in remembrance of three of her sisters, namely Charlotte Maria Hoby who died on 19 April 1837, Sarah Parker who died on 30 August 1877 and Augusta Mary on 25 November 1887.

8

George Henry William Alderson

Little is known about the early life of George Henry William Alderson, my great grandfather. He was the eldest son of Jonathan Alderson from his second marriage to Georgiana, née Taylor. He went to Rossall School and, with his brother Frank, kept a gig there. Stories passed down by the family suggest that George was something of an adventurer. He served in the Royal Navy, presumably during the 1860s, and is said to have visited Siberia but for what purpose is anyone's guess. On 13 February 1872 he married Emily Laura Stevenson Bellairs, one of the thirteen children of Rev Charles Bellairs and Anna Maria Bradshaw-Isherwood. They were married at Charles Bellairs' church of Sutton-in-Ashfield in Nottinghamshire. George's profession was given as "Esquire" and his residence as the Manor House, Allesley in Warwickshire.

The happy couple departed almost immediately for Canada and settled at Port Rowan on Lake Erie in Ontario. Here Emily gave birth to three boys, Francis Bellairs born on 11 May 1873, Charles Henry on 18 April 1876 and William Seaforth, my grandfather, on 3 April 1878. Port Rowan is in Walsingham Township, Norfolk County and on their birth certificates their

George Henry William Alderson

father is referred to as "G. H. W. Alderson, Esq., Gentleman of Port Rowan." Port Rowan overlooks Long Point Bay, mid way between Niagara and Windsor, on the north shore of the lake. It is a small and pretty place where boating, swimming, fishing, bird watching, golf and tennis are popular visitor pursuits. It would have been smaller still in the 1870s, but surrounded then, as now, by rich farming country, tomatoes and tobacco being main crops.

The family then moved to Little Current on Manitoulin Island, in northern Lake Huron, and here, on 17 November 1880, a fourth son was born. His birth was registered as George Burris Alderson at Howland Township in Algoma County and father is now recorded as a "farmer" and JP (Justice of the Peace).

Emily
Laura
Stevenson Bellairs

Baby George had many name variations during his life time, and was usually known as Christopher. Burris is a very strange name in the Alderson litany and is likely to be a mistake for Ennis, this being the name given to his great great grandmother, Mary Ennis Read and to Mary's father and grandfather. Perhaps a busy registrar was unable to read the handwriting presented to him, or possibly it was misread from the original parish registers. Christopher might have been omitted simply because it contravened the North American convention of only recognising two Christian names, or perhaps it was added in later life? Certainly he was consistently known as Kit.

The 1881 census for Ontario lists the whole family, George aged 39, farmer, Emily aged 33, Frank aged eight, Charles five, William three and George nine months, living in District 182, Algoma, sub-district "A," Howland Township, line 9, house 73. All are Church of England and the enumeration date was 28 June 1881.

Why did they move from Port Rowan to Manitoulin Island, one

wonders? It would have been a long journey in the late 19th century. They would first have travelled the 160 miles from Port Rowan overland to Owen Sound from where they would have caught a boat to take them across Georgian Bay in Lake Huron to Little Current, another 120 miles. Perhaps the gentleman of Port Rowan needed some income and so became the farmer of Little Current?

Little Current is a small town with a big history. The port now caters mainly for the thousands of pleasure craft that visit from other parts of Canada and the United States, but in the 19th century it was a significant commercial port. Thousands of tons of timber passed through on the way to the USA, including that from which Chicago was re-built following the devastating fire of 1871. In the other direction coal came from Pennsylvania for the great nickel furnaces of Sudbury, for which in 1913 a railway was built to take it there from Little Current.

The first European to set foot in Manitoulin was Samuel de Champlain in 1603, cartographer and explorer and later Governor of New France. Manitoulin means "spirit" and the island is believed to be the home of the Great Spirit Kitchie Manitou in Ojibwe Indian legend. It forms part of the Canadian Shield, with granite and quartz to the north and lime-stone to the south. Manitoulin, some 80 miles long yet as narrow as two miles in places, is claimed to be the largest fresh water island in the world. It contains 900 species of flora, one fifth of Canada's total, and is very beautiful.

George and his family lived three miles out of Little Current on White's Point, a mile-long tree-lined peninsula running into the North Channel. On a smaller promontory, that they named Alderson's Point, they moved into an old farmhouse called The Hermitage. It was report-ed that "Quite often they entertained people from the village." Manitoulin Island was neither the best nor the worst of places to farm though it might have been difficult competing with the richer pastures of Southern Ontario.

Canada is a land of vast open spaces and as George and his family looked out from the front door of The Hermitage great vistas would have welcomed them every morning. The wide expanse of the lake is framed by forests of pine and birch leading to the horizon in every direction, the hot summer sun cooled by a breeze from the lake, whereas in winter the ice and snow shimmer in the clear air. Travel was by sledge drawn by a team of eight dogs.

There were few colonists in the immediate vicinity but the family was part of a happy community. The only other children the boys knew and played with were Indians and they were particularly fond of an adult brave named Windybush, as was their father, for George appointed Windybush his butler and the children's nurse and tutor.

It was decided that there should be a jail at Little Current and, as George was the only magistrate on Manitoulin Island, it was his task to have it built. It was the first stone building on the island. There was no one to incarcerate in the new edifice, until Windybush, of all people, obliged by stealing some hens. He was caught in the hen house wearing the splendid top hat, originally from Lock's of St James Street in London, that George had given him. His master had the unfortunate task of sending his much loved servant to prison for 28 days.

Emily and her four sons would take food to Windybush every day and, according to my Great Uncle Charles, he and his brothers would climb in via a hole in the roof and stay the night in jail with their friend. George was aware of this and heaved a mighty sigh of relief when Windybush was released, for had his sons been caught, or Windybush escaped, he would have had some explaining to do. The prison survives, in good condition, and is the size of a large garage, but without a purpose and looking rather incongruous, situated between two suburban gardens.

The Canadian adventure appears to have come to an abrupt end for we read in a letter from his brother, the Rev Frank Alderson, to another relative, dated St Thomas Day (21 December) 1881 "You will probably be astonished to hear that my brother George from Canada is now staying with me: he will be in England for the next few weeks so that it would be well to get matters settled if possible before he leaves." The catalyst for the return home is probably the law suit, (the same that led to the sale of Highfield Terrace), in which the family is said to have lost £1 million to the Rimington-Wilsons, a branch of the Wilson family referred to in the previous chapter. The case appears to have hung on the interpretation of a will, eventually settled in the House of Lords, the costs alone amounting to £80,000, a fortune in itself at that time.

Presumably George returned to Canada to bring the family home. It is said that when Rev. Frank went to Liverpool to meet his brother and nephews off the boat, he recognised the cry of George, calling "Porter, porter, carry my bags!" He then saw George and four small boys, lined up against a dockside warehouse, relieving themselves!

We have little information about how George and Emily spent the last 30 years of their lives. They moved back to North Derbyshire and lived at Brimington, near Chesterfield. George was an accomplished amateur cabinet maker and examples of his work remain with the family. As a Justice of the Peace he would have had formal duties to undertake and he was likely to have been involved with the church. He occasionally stayed at a farm on the Ulley estate. The lintel over the farmhouse door is inscribed 1648. It was a former rotten borough and George would shoot with Lord Rosebery, who in 1894 would tell his circle, he became Prime Minister, won the Derby and married a Rothschild, the richest heiress in the world!

Emily Bellairs had an eccentric streak about her and photographs show her as a fearsome woman, not to be encountered lightly. She is said to have only employed people with one leg and the coachman proved the point. On one occasion the Duke of Portland came to lunch and Emily, knowing him to be a keen horticulturist, showed him some rare Japanese fronds she had in her garden and promised to send him some cuttings. Her eccentricity took the better of her and instead she sent the duke a box of kippers, implying that he should plant the bones and that the fronds would emerge!

Both Emily and George died in 1911, Emily at Margate in Kent in July aged 65 and George aged 69 at Droylesden, near Manchester in October. What Emily was doing in Margate is anybody's guess but George was probably visiting his youngest son, Kit, who lived in Manchester.

~ ~ ~ ~ ~ ~ ~ ~ ~ ~ ~ ~ ~ ~

George's elder half brother, William Marmaduke Dixwell Alderson (1835-1877), the son of Jonathan and Isabella Newsham, was the only one of Captain Jonathan Alderson's four sons to follow him into the army, becoming a captain in the Queen's Royal Regiment. On 1st January 1857 he married Josephine Spear, daughter of Rev. John Joseph Spear of Parkhurst on the Isle of Wight. Josephine lived well into the 20th century, being in her 90s when she died in 1927. Presumably it was from the Newsham family that the name Marmaduke was introduced to the Aldersons, clearly a name with staying power, for William and Josephine passed it on to their elder son, and he in turn to his, and it was from these second cousins that my parents thought it suitable to bring across to me!

William and Josephine had two sons, Marmaduke Jonathan George Alderson (1864-1925) and Augustus Dixwell Alderson (1868-1944).

Marmaduke Jonathan George married Ethel Byrde and was variously of Gannow Hill, in Derbyshire, Tickhill in Yorkshire and also of Gannow Hill in Shropshire, presumably the same as that of his half-Uncle Frank referred to below. He left Peterhouse, Cambridge without graduating in 1888 and became a coffee planter in Ceylon and was a Major in the RASC during the Great War. Marmaduke and Ethel had three sons.

Their eldest son, Marmaduke Guy Alderson, inherited his father's estates in Ceylon. The second son, Dixwell Alderson, was killed in action aboard *HMS Conqueror* in 1917. The third son, Marmaduke Jonathan Roland Alderson, married Joan Branfoot and was a distinguished airline pilot with Imperial Airways, and later BOAC. They had two sons and a daughter and live variously in Somerset and Sussex.

Augustus Dixwell Alderson was of Emmanuel College and Ridley Hall, Cambridge and was vicar of Tickhill in Yorkshire from 1899 and of Todwick in the same county from 1933-1939. He married Wilhelmina Lillingston in 1897 and they had issue.

George's full brother, Frank, also went to Rossall and to Christ's College, Cambridge. He was ordained by the Bishop of Norwich in 1869 and the same year became curate of Burnham Sutton in Norfolk. In 1873 he became curate at Bodenham in Herefordshire and the following year moved to a similar position in Dudleston in northern Shropshire, becoming vicar there in 1877. He restored the parish church but had to resign the living in 1888 due to a throat infection. He then lived at The Mount in Oswestry before, in 1894, moving to an enormous 33 room mansion that the family had built at Welsh Frankton, three miles south of Dudleston and mid way between Oswestry and Ellesmere. This great pile has commanding views and was named Gannow Hill, after the farm of the same name in Derbyshire, as also was the village that grew up around it, as current maps confirm. Frank lived in style and employed full staff at Gannow Hill. It was here that he died on 15 November 1900. He is buried at Welsh Frankton.

Frank Alderson married his cousin, Augusta, the youngest daughter of soldier Jonathan Alderson's elder brother, Christopher and his wife Georgiana Peel. Did Frank and Augusta have issue? There is no mention in the press reports of children attending Frank's funeral but on a visit there in 1980 the author was told by the verger's wife that they had one daughter who married a soldier called Morris. No record, however, has been found.

In March 1914, Aunt Augusta, the Rev. Frank Alderson's widow, wrote to her nephew William Seaforth Alderson about passing over some family silver and was concerned that William would have to pay tax because some of it was crested. "So far as I can make out licences were only taken out in January so you would not have to worry about it this year. I would most gladly have sent the half guinea but I have had grievous losses and cannot make both ends meet - I never thought of drawing you into any expense by the gift of silver but I have been ill for months and unable to exercise my full judgement. Had you already been using the crest of course there would have been no further tax, nor would the mere possession of it - only the use - entail cost." But "P.S. I ought to have said that every article having crest on is liable to tax whether for use or ornament." Most of this silver remains with the family to this day, though fortunately the "crest" tax no longer has to be paid!

9

Charles Bellairs

We now turn to the family of Emily Bellairs, George Henry William Alderson's wife. Emily's father was Charles Bellairs, my great great grandfather.

The Bellairs family home was Deeping St Nicholas in Lincolnshire though Charles Bellairs was born at Oxford in 1818. He was the third son and fourth child of Henry Bellairs and Dorothy Parker Mackenzie.

In 1837 Charles became an undergraduate at Worcester College, Oxford and in graphic detail recorded in his diary how he ingratiated himself with his fellow freshers. "Being the younger son of a country clergyman I went there on a small allowance but was determined not to lower myself by making inferior acquaintances. I soon became friendly with the best men of the College, amongst whom was a young lad, the only son of a county gentleman in Cheshire whose income I afterwards understood was about £5000 a year and who resided in an old mansion where his ancestors had flourished for many years. I was told that he was considered peculiar but that the old squire was mighty respected and a great favourite with his tenants and dependents."

Charles soon became "intimate with this specimen of the forward class who wore silk instead of worsted." This specimen was Thomas, son of John Bradshaw-Isherwood of Marple Hall in Cheshire. Charles learned that Tom had three unmarried sisters and he was soon invited to visit Marple.

The coach was sent to meet him at Manchester. "We had a drive of 11 miles, accomplished in about an hour and a half. We entered the shabby looking park, without much ornamental timber, by a handsome pair of wooden gates and I saw at once that it was an ample Elizabeth mansion. The door was opened by a stately middle-aged butler in black who seemed as if the place had been made for him and he for the place. He informed me that his master would be pleased to see me in the oak parlour. He opened the door and announced my name to the squire. An old gentleman between 60 and 70 rose to receive me. He was rather stout and rosy and wore a blue coat with brass buttons, a grey waistcoat and dark trousers, and a heavy gold chain with two enormous seals hanging from the watch pocket. He had the smallest hands and feet I ever saw."

The old man apologised for the absence of Tom, ill in bed, and lamented that "He is my only son, and it is of great importance that he should live till he is of age, for the property is strictly entailed and if he should die before he is 21, it will go to the Salwin family and not to my daughters. I have directed my lawyers to get everything ready against his coming of age and the very moment the clock strikes 12 Sir, this disagreeable entail will be cut off, so I hope he will get better. I have the principal physician to see him every other day from Manchester, whose fee is six guineas."

The squire then introduced Charles to his daughters. Anna Maria, he reported "is fond of riding spirited horses. She is the God-daughter of the Rector of Stockport, after whose sister she is named." We learn that the squire's wife played the organ in the drawing room and "is frequently away at the sea side but I have so many home occupations I do not much miss her."

"As there were four young ladies in the house [the girls plus the vicar's wife] and I was the only young gentleman, I probably took some pains with my toilette [for dinner]. The four damsels all dressed in plain but becoming white dresses with bouquets of flowers. The vicar (he was invited if the squire approved of Sunday's sermon) and his wife arrived,

Marple Hall

and dinner was announced "and we all walked in state to the other end of the hall, past coats-of-arms of those families who were connected to the Bradshaw-Isherwoods from the time of Henry VIII and George III, and entered the dining room. The old gentleman was extremely polite and courteous to everybody, except his daughters, whom he snubbed on every occasion, admonishing them with "girls, hold your tongues."

The following day the squire attended the Annual Meeting of the Agricultural Society in Manchester and from which he had received no less than 26 medals for tree planting and rearing cows and sheep. It would be remiss of him not to wear them, he explained, but added with some relief that he was not obliged to wear the dishes, salvers and cups he had won for trotting matches, ploughing and other things.

On a tour of the house Charles was shown "what is vulgarly called by my wife King Charles Closet. I do not at all approve of it myself, but I have to put up with many things. I have not told you before, Sir, that my wife is of a very romantic turn, and it frequently leads her to excess, as in the fitting up of this closet. That extraordinary and indeed ludicrous figure on its knees in the centre is intended for the martyred Charles I, and he is supposed to be kneeling before that table perusing his Death Warrant. You are perhaps not aware that Judge Bradshaw, who presided at his trial, was born in this house, and that I am descended from his eldest brother. I am not proud of the connection, Sir."

An invitation from Sir Salisbury Davenport to a dinner party at nearby Bramhall Hall was the excuse, if one be needed, for Squire Bradshaw-Isherwood to impart to Charles how "he grieved to think he must be living beyond his income. I believe his estate is mortgaged ....and as he lives at much greater expense than I do I am afraid he is, at times, inconvenienced." He bemoaned the fact that his eldest brother

Charles
Bellairs

had had to sell 1000 acres of the Marple estate because "he was too fond of horses and dogs." Further, he ventured, "If I had married Lady Davenport, as I believe I might have done, there would have been twice 1000 acres added to the estate." He pointed out, however, that he would not have had to take her name, as Sir Salisbury did, "for my family is as old as hers, and as I already have two surnames, I do not think I could have been expected to take a third."

We learn that the Squire had been High Sheriff, presumably of Cheshire, in the year that peace was made with France [1815]. He was a keen churchman. He paid marked attention to Sunday's sermon and would rise in his pew and take note of who was absent from church.

Charles closes his diary by recording: "I overheard the old gentleman tell Lady Davenport that he was pleased with his son's College friend, that I was respectful and not over talkative, for it was agreeable to find a young man in the present day who knew how to behave to his elders."

On his death bed in 1839, the old man told Anna Maria, his eldest daughter, to marry Charles and this she did in December of the same year. The following year, Tom Bradshaw-Isherwood married Charles' sister, Mary Ellen Bellairs. In 1840, it was Mary who, with babe in arms, dismissed a rioting Chartist mob from the door of Marple Hall by employing a firm hand allied with profound reasoning. Eventually the rebel leaders were heard to say: "The Misses is reet, lads, let's let her alone." The courage and fortitude that she showed on this occasion were used by Disraeli in his novel *Sybil.*

The story of Charles wooing Anna Maria is amusingly recounted in the biography of his parents *Kathleen and Frank* by Christopher Isherwood, a great grandson of Thomas and Mary Ellen Bradshaw-Isherwood. The name was hyphenated when Mary, the last of the Bradshaws, married Nathaniel Isherwood, a felt maker from Bolton in Lancashire. Christopher, however, considered hyphenated names pretentious and dropped the Bradshaw. To compensate, he gave it to the autobiographical character of his *Berlin Stories*, together with his other Christian name, thus William Bradshaw. In 1955 the *Berlin Stories* were made into the film *I Am A Camera* and later into the musical *Cabaret* and, in 1972, the film of the same name, for which Liza Minnelli won acclaim and an Oscar.

Charles was ordained deacon in 1841 and priest by the Bishop of Worcester in 1843. Shortly afterwards he became curate to his father at

Bedworth, a position he held until 1861, with the exception of a short period from 1844 when he was perpetual curate of Christ Church in adjoining Coventry. Eighteen years a curate to his father might suggest a lack of ambition but this stands uneasily with the wooing of his wife. In any event there could have been few better teachers than Henry Bellairs.

In 1861, on the nomination of Rev. Henry Glynne, Mrs Gladstone's brother, Charles moved to Flintshire to take up his duties as perpetual curate of Buckley Mountain in the parish of Harwarden, a position he held for four years.

Charles then moved to Sutton-in-Ashfield, near Mansfield in Nottinghamshire where, under the patronage of the Duke of Devonshire, he became vicar in 1867. It was here that he was to make his mark as the Established Church broke out of the shackles of Georgian privilege and somnolence to espouse the Victorian ethos and embrace the rising generations of the industrial revolution. The press cuttings tell us that, almost immediately, Charles was in the thick of restoring and enlarging the church, building a school and founding a mission chapel.

Charles certainly made things happen for, a mere five months after his arrival, the foundation stone was laid for a new school for 300 children

Sutton-in-Ashfield Church, Nottinghamshire.

at Hucknall-under-Huthwaite, a township of 3,000 people within the parish of Sutton. Prior to this the Wesleyan churches provided the only means of education in Hucknall, but they were happy enough to share in the celebrations, bringing no less than 300 children and a drum and fife band to help make the day a gay occasion. The Dowager Countess of Carnarvon had donated the land and £400 towards the building of the school. At the unveiling Charles asked that Lady Carnarvon's life be spared to enable her "to see the children grow up to be well behaved and obedient to their sovereign." One hopes the children obliged, for Sutton was a tough parish, the most difficult in his diocese in the opinion of the Bishop of Lincoln.

The main trade in Sutton was hand loom weaving but there was considerable poverty and local people had been involved in the burning of Nottingham Castle during the reform riots some years earlier. The green Chartist flag was still brought out and paraded at election time. Education was the key to enlightenment and the building of schools was the way. When Charles arrived in Sutton baptism was largely unheard of among the working people. He undertook no less than 1608 baptisms in his first year, 800 in his second and more than 600 in his third. The parish registers show that on one occasion he baptised 70 children in one day.

Charles was soon hard at work putting Sutton-in-Ashfield Church "in a different condition from the years of neglect." He had the church restored, had north and south aisles added and had the unsightly galleries removed. At the re-dedication he said "It is now a great relief to be free from the necessity of begging" but immediately set to work begging again, this time for funds to build a school at Forrest-side, another part of the parish, with a population of 1500 people. "It would be a dreadful reflection on the wealth and intelligence of the neighbourhood" he said "if this were not to be done."

We hear much today about climate change, but gales and storms are not a new phenomenon. In December 1873 gales brought Charles Bellairs' dining room extension at Sutton Vicarage crashing down. Presumably it was as sturdily built as any Victorian edifice but that did not prevent the chimney from falling with a tremendous crash, leaving the entire structure a mass of ruins, every piece of furniture smashed to atoms, leaving a sad scene of desolation.

In 1874 the Duke of Devonshire moved Charles to Bolton Abbey, that romantic pile set in lush green fields alongside the River Wharfe in Yorkshire, with the majesty of the Yorkshire dales behind it.

The Augustinian Priory of Bolton was founded in 1155 and was dissolved by Henry VIII in 1539. The Dissolution of the Monasteries was a messy business and the Yorkshire rising known as the Pilgrimage of Grace was savagely suppressed by Henry. Nearby Skipton Castle was besieged. It was defended by the Earl of Cumberland and, unable to gain entrance, the King's attackers decided to seize the Earl's wife and children from Bolton Priory, where they had been placed for safe keeping. They had intended to rape them beneath the castle walls until it submitted. Fortunately for the ladies this dastardly plot was foiled as Bolton itself surrendered just in time. After the Dissolution, however, the King was good enough to allow the Priory Chapel to become a church to serve the local population, placing it under the jurisdiction of Skipton. The estate was eventually purchased for £2,490 by Henry Clifford, that same Earl of Cumberland.

As the years passed the priests in charge gradually took on more responsibility and, in the 19th century they embarked upon substantial restoration of the church. In 1864 Bolton became an independent parish with a rector of its own and the second of these was Charles. His patron, the 7th Duke of Devonshire, was a direct descendant of Henry Clifford, who 300 years earlier had acquired the estate.

The name Abbey is a misnomer, for a priory it certainly was and a parish church it now is, but an abbey it has never been. It is thought that it takes its name from the railway station which was named Abbey by a confused railway official, a non-believer perhaps! This took place in Charles' day but either he was not consulted or perhaps he was happy to turn a blind eye to a romantic deception!

Charles saw the rebuilding of the east wall in 1877 and the decoration of the beautiful stone reredos, painted by a local artist, George Bottomley, in 1880. It contains eleven panels depicting ecclesiastical symbols, including those of the joint patrons of the church, the lily, symbol of the Blessed Virgin Mary and St Cuthbert's Cross.

As at Sutton-in-Ashfield, Charles quickly set to work. The registers contain a list of names, including those of many adults, below which is written, "These sixty I baptised this day," signed Charles Bellairs. We learn also that in 1878 Charles opened both a day school and a Sunday School at nearby Barden Moor.

It was during Charles' time at Bolton that the Phoenix Park murders took place. The Duke's son, Lord Frederick Cavendish, was appointed Chief Secretary for Ireland in 1882. He arrived in Dublin two days later, on 6 May, and he and his Under Secretary were stabbed to death as they walked to their residence in Phoenix Park. This was the first murder of a public figure since that of Prime Minister Spencer Perceval 70 years earlier and caused outrage in both Britain and Ireland.

Charles Bellairs chaired a meeting in the Boyle Room at Bolton at which

Cavendish Monument, Bolton Abbey

two resolutions were passed, the first expressing to the duke a sharing with "the whole nation the feeling of horror which has deprived your grace of a son ....and the Queen of a courageous and unselfish servant." The second was addressed to Lady Cavendish expressing "sorrow shared by every man, woman and child in this parish.... of the noble and unselfish and useful life.... died as a true martyr in the service of his Queen and country.... praying that you be supported in your life long bereavement." These were signed by Charles. On 11 May he conducted a memorial service in the Abbey and later had a monument erected in memory of Cavendish, a truly splendid pile, well looked after to the present day.

The Boyle Room is named after Robert Boyle, himself an Irishman, famous for Boyle's Law of physics of 1762. Boyle had left monies for the establishment of a school, which was originally housed in what in Charles' day was his rectory, which is situated alongside the Priory.

In June a midsummer parish party was held at Bolton, an annual event no doubt. The amusements commenced at 12 o'clock with a cricket match between the married and single, the latter winning, by what margin we do not know. At 2 o'clock there was a short service in the Abbey with some hearty hymns and an address from the rector based on the Bible story of Elisha and the children of Jericho. At 4 o'clock 138 children sat down to an excellent meat tea in the Boyle room, and at 5 o'clock 200 parishioners partook of tea and sandwiches. After tea, presents were distributed to the children on the lawn and then the sports started, embracing steeple chases, jumping in sacks, high jump, throwing the cricket ball and more. The grand finale was a donkey race and the fun continued until dark when everyone went home happy and exhausted.

One rather nebulous story that has survived about Charles is that he invested in a candle factory in Liverpool, and would rub his hands in glee at Catholic emancipation, as the influx of Irish immigrants would improve the trade!

The last position held by Charles was at Goadby Marwood, near Melton Mowbray in Leicestershire. He retired to Grantham in Lincolnshire in 1888, and there he died in 1890. Charles Bellairs and Anna Maria Bradshaw-Isherwood had seven sons and four daughters, each of the sons going to a different college at Oxford.

~ ~ ~ ~ ~ ~ ~ ~ ~ ~ ~ ~ ~ ~

Charles' eldest brother, Henry Walford Bellairs, was Vicar of Nuneaton and Canon of Worcester Cathedral and he founded Cheltenham Ladies College, where his portrait may be seen. Charles' younger brother, George Byng Bellairs, had seven daughters. The eldest, Dora Ennis Bellairs, married Reginald Simpson Graham and together with their daughter, also Dora Ennis, embarked on a trip of exploration of the Amazon. Unfortunately, in 1845, they were all drowned. Memorials were erected to them in Bedworth Church.

The second daughter, Mary Ellen Bellairs, married Thomas Bradshaw-Isherwood as mentioned above.

The third daughter, Rosemira, married Benjamin Lancaster, a man who had acquired considerable wealth. He had been clerk to a Russian Mercantile business but the source of his fortune was investments in New Zealand.

Lancaster had been heavily influenced by the High-Anglican Oxford Movement into which he poured money to enable the building of churches and to help alleviate the disadvantaged in poverty stricken parts of London. Rosemira had been shocked to find, so near the fashionable parts of the capital, degradation even worse than that with which she was familiar in Bedworth. A Sisterhood was established and particularly impressive was the church of St Augustine at Kilburn, now in north London, but then on the leafy outskirts.

Lancaster had invested in land in Christchurch, which became known as the Lancaster Estate. On 28 July 1881 a cricket club was established and part of the estate was acquired for the ground. The first match was arranged for 8 October 1881 - but it rained. Today, Lancaster Park is the New Zealand Test Match Cricket ground and also where the All Blacks play many of their rugby internationals.

10

Henry Bellairs "The Great" - Sailor, Soldier, Priest

Charles' father was Henry Bellairs, known in the family as "Henry the Great." He was born at Stamford in Lincolnshire on 29 August 1790 and was educated at Uppingham School.

Henry hero-worshiped Nelson, who came from north Norfolk on the other side of the Wash, and in 1805 he joined the Royal Navy as a first-class volunteer on board *HMS Spartiate*, under the command of Sir F. Laforey, Bart. He also became acquainted with Lady Hamilton and had a boyish admiration for her beauty and was a frequent visitor to her house.

Nelson took Henry under his wing and, at the start of the Battle of Trafalgar, under conditions of considerable danger, Henry delivered a private message to Nelson on board the *Victory*. Years afterwards he would tell that whenever he thought of that momentous day he could still feel Nelson's reassuring hand on his shoulder.

HMS Spartiate had a crew of 640 men and Henry was a fifteen year old midshipman as Nelson pursued the Combined Fleet to the West Indies and back and then entered into battle at Trafalgar. *Spartiate* was a large two decker of 74 guns (a third rate) and had been built for the French fleet at Toulon as Le Spatiate in 1797. Within a year she was captured from the French at the bloody Battle of the Nile (or Aboukir Bay), presumably on her first outing in anger. Sailors likened her to a witch and claimed she must have been built of stolen timber for she sailed better by night than by day. After Trafalgar she became a sheer hulk, a floating crane, at Plymouth before eventually being broken up in 1857.

As a midshipman, Henry would have been responsible for one of the ship's cannon and its crew of six men. *Spartiate* was the rearmost ship in Nelson's division at Trafalgar and played a decisive part in the battle, disabling *Formidable*, the flagship of Admiral Demonair who command-ed the van of the Combined Fleet. *Spartiate* passed within point blank range of her and fired a broadside into her bows below the water line which virtually crippled her. She then engaged four other French ships in turn. She cut off the Spanish ship *Neptuno*, 84 guns, got alongside her and after an hour's fighting forced her to surrender. *Spartiate* had her foretopsail shot away and her masts, yards and rigging were a good deal damaged. Five men were killed and twenty wounded, among the latter being Henry who was wounded both in the arm and the leg. He afterwards received a sword from the Patriotic Fund and a Medal from the Admiralty.

Henry left the Navy in 1808 and, in the intervening months before joining the Army, he made himself useful by learning the trades of carpenter, blacksmith and cobbler in turn and was soon to boast that he could make a shoe as well as his teacher.

In November 1808 Henry, now eighteen, purchased a commission as Cornet in the 15th Light Dragoons, later the 15th Hussars. He travelled from Stamford to Dorchester to join the Regiment. He went, however, not as the dashing young officer that he was, but rather as his servant, for he dressed in his groom's livery and installed the groom in his coach. Thus Henry travelled halfway across England as his own groom with the led horse, later explaining that he had gained much useful experience by it.

In 1810 Henry's regiment was posted to Hounslow in Middlesex, and there he met sixteen year old Dorothy Parker Mackenzie, the daughter of Peter Mackenzie and his wife Mary Ennis Read of Grove House, Twickenham and of Harmony Hall, Jamaica. Henry and Dorothy instantly fell in love but there was parental opposition to a match.

Henry's reputation as an eighteen year old daredevil officer had preceded him and the Napoleonic wars were still raging. He was banned from seeing Dorothy. Not so easily brushed aside, Henry disguised himself as a footman in order to meet her whilst serving at dinner and at balls. He would hand the ladies out of their carriage, undetected, except by his loved one, whose hand he would clasp and into whose eyes he would catch a quick loving glance.

Eventually Henry's subterfuge was discovered but the love birds had their way, though not until he had acquiesced to Mackenzie's demand that he leave the Army. They were married at Twickenham Parish Church in March 1811. They lived at Grove House for a year or so before moving to a cottage in Devonshire. There Dorothy, an accomplished musician, would play on her high grand piano and give small recitals to guests who would listen spellbound to her singing Welsh airs and playing the harp.

Henry was a keen sportsman and one day he winged a pheasant but it scrambled through the hedge into the next field, which was owned by a neighbour. Henry crawled through the hedge to pick it up, when he saw the gamekeeper hurrying towards him. Always one for a joke, Henry turned up his collar, pulled down his cap, puffed out his cheeks and affected a hideous squint and stood his ground. The keeper was in a great rage and demanded Henry's name and address. A summons followed but when Henry appeared before the magistrate the keeper exclaimed "This ain't the man I found poaching for he was the ugliest man I ever clapped eyes on." But Henry insisted that he was the man. The confused magistrate had no option but to dismiss the case. Afterwards, Henry met the gamekeeper outside the court and again transformed himself into the uncouth "poacher," and with a wink squeezed some silver into his quivering hand.

In 1814 Henry and Dorothy lived at the Manor House at Freshford in Somerset for a short time and it was here that Henry decided to enter the church. He matriculated at St Mary's Hall, Oxford in July 1817 and became curate, and later priest, of Radley in Berkshire. Two years later, in September 1819, he became curate of Bedworth in Warwickshire and it was here that Henry was to undertake his life's work. The living was under sequestration, the irresponsible incumbent, who happened to be the son of the patron, having fled abroad to Ceylon. Ten years later the absent 'incumbent' died and a contrivance was then entered into to ensure that Henry became Rector of Bedworth, a position he held until he resigned the living in 1864, 45 years after his arrival.

When Henry came to Bedworth the parish was devastated. The church was dilapidated, congregations were small and the schools were such in name alone. By the time he departed he had brought about a transformation. Henry had also been strongly influenced by the Oxford Movement and he had the zeal of the missionary about him. Soon the church had doubled in size, the congregation was overflowing and the schools were full and properly organised.

Henry brought this transformation about by force of personality, courageous and judicious management and by a genuine concern for his parishioners. Bedworth was heavily dependent on the ribbon weaving industry and was as poor as any town in the country, having been severely damaged by the recession which followed the peace of Waterloo. Many of its inhabitants lived lives of exhaustion and impoverishment.

Shortly after his arrival, Henry came across a commotion in the Market Square and upon investigation found, in the centre of a large throng, two women, partially stripped, fighting. He was about to separate them when a powerfully built man stepped forward, saying "Parson, what business have you to interfere?" and struck Henry a blow on the face. The new curate, 6ft. 2in. tall, immediately struck back and gave the miner both a sound thrashing and the shock of his life. He then addressed the crowd with some plain speaking. He won them round, and was rewarded with hearty cheers and their respect for ever afterwards, for his intervention that day. Henry believed that this incident did more to transform Bedworth than any sermon he ever preached, and he never again received an uncivil word from a parishioner in all the years that he was there.

Henry was an eloquent preacher who held his vast congregations spellbound. His wild escapades now behind him, he remained a jovial and popular character with the common touch. He was a good looking man and his stature gave him a natural air of authority, almost that of the local squire. He worked incessantly to improve the lives of his flock and would visit the public houses late at night where immorality, gambling and drunkenness were common.

Dorothy gave her children a treasured upbringing at Bedworth Rectory for which there is no better testament than that crafted years later by her daughter, Laura: "Twelve of us were reared to be men and women in the dear, picturesque, moated old Rectory. My brother Charles was for twenty years the devoted fellow worker with my father, and, although we have been scattered about in various counties, and become acquainted with diverse parishes, we all agreed that we had never found the love, respect and gratitude we had invariably for so

Henry Bellairs as Rector of Bedworth, 1857

77

many years received from our dear friends at Bedworth." Dorothy died in 1857 and is buried at St Giles, Exhall, two miles north of Bedworth.

In 1853 Henry was installed as honourary Canon of Worcester Cathedral. In 1864 he retired to Devon. He died at Paignton in 1872 aged 81 and lies alongside his beloved wife Dorothy, so near his spiritual home of Bedworth. There he is remembered by Bellairs Avenue and by the Henry Bellairs Church of England Middle School.

Nona, the only one of Henry's and Dorothy's children not to marry, also left her mark on Bedworth. In the 1850s there was a slump in the weaving industry, the only source of employment, and the consequences were dire for the population. The inhabitants were starving, the children wore rags and charity just about kept them alive. The only hope was escape to the colonies, but how to pay for a long sea voyage and to where?

Nona begged, borrowed and cajoled friends and some of the wealthier townspeople for donations to send starving families abroad, mainly to Australia. She thus saved the lives of many, whose moving accounts of Nona's drive to help them, and of the new lives they were able to lead, are a joyous testimony to her heroic efforts.

~~~~~~~~~~~~~~~

The Rectory, Bedworth.

Henry Bellairs was the third of the four sons of Abel Walford Bellairs. The eldest was James, born at Uffington in 1782. He married Elizabeth Ann, daughter of Lawrence Peel of Ardwick, Lancashire and niece of Sir Robert Peel. In 1845 he assumed by sign-manual the name and arms of Stevenson instead of Bellairs, in compliance with the will of his cousin, William Stevenson.

The second son was George Bellairs. He married Mary, daughter of Samuel Linwood, and they named their eldest son, born in 1825, Stevenson Gilbert. He later became Rector of Goadby Marwood.

Henry the Great was not so enamoured with the Stevensons as not one of his thirteen children was given that name, but his son Charles resurrected it by appending it to his tenth child, namely my great grandmother, Emily Laura Stevenson Bellairs.

The fourth son was William, later Sir William, who was a Captain in the 15th Hussars and who saw action in the Peninsular War and at Waterloo.

11

Abel Walford Bellairs

Henry's father was Abel Walford Bellairs who was born in 1755 in the Deepings, a series of scattered villages between Stamford and Spalding in Lincolnshire, through which the River Welland flows on its slow and flat journey through Deeping Fen and into the Wash. He died in Derbyshire in 1839. In 1781 he married Susanna Lowley, daughter of Miles Lowley of Oakham in Rutland. Susanna died in 1823 and is buried at Bedworth.

Abel Walford Bellairs was a man of influence. He was High Sheriff of Rutland and Deputy Lord Lieutenant of Lincolnshire and, we are told, of Northamptonshire too. His claim to fame for us, however, is that he changed the family name by inserting the "i" in Bellairs, for his father was James Bellars of Uffington, near Stamford, who married Mary, daughter of Abel Walford.

Abel Walford Bellairs's other claim to fame is that he was a banker, firstly in Stamford and later, in 1803 in Melton Mowbray and Derby. The bank financed estates and farms in the East Midland counties and some of the new industries that were springing up in the age of steam.

Note from Abel Walford Bellairs' Stamford Bank

We know that during the next ten years the bank paid a subscription to the Lincoln Asylum, that Abel Walford's Game Duty was paid, that an account was handled on behalf of the Relief of Russian Sufferers and another for the Relief of Married Lying-in Women in Stamford. Then came the crash.

On Monday 8 July 1814 the bank at Stamford closed after an hour and a half of trading. The following day the Leicestershire bank folded, followed by that in Derby on the Wednesday. On 22 July our hero was declared bankrupt. The assignees sold his house and furniture in September, a sale which "drew a respectable company." And so it should have, for Abel Walford's house in Stamford remains to this day a splendid four-storey Georgian house built from the beautiful mellow yellow stone that makes Stamford one of the loveliest towns in England.

In 1815 Abel Walford's creditors were paid a first installment of 7/6 in the pound. This was followed by another pay out of 10d and a final dividend of 1d in 1833, a total pay out of approximately 43%. In 1839, probably to coincide with his death, it was reported that "many were ruined by failure of his banks in Stamford, Leicestershire and Derby."

12

d'Albini and Bellars

Let us now take a quick look at the origins of the Bellars. Prior to the Conquest the home of the Bellars family was in Albenaye, to use modern spelling, in Normandy. Nigel d'Albini, married Amicia de Guerche, whose brother, the Earl of Northumberland, made a name for himself by slaying King Malcolm of Scotland in 1095. Their second son, Nigel d'Albini, was bow bearer to William Rufus and was distinguished for his valour and military skill, for which in 1095 the King rewarded him with large possessions in England. He founded the Priory of Axholme, (his elder brother William having founded Wymondham Abbey in Norfolk) and lived to a good age as a monk in Rouen, where he died.

He managed to divorce his first wife, not because they were married during her first husband's lifetime, but because of sanguinity. In 1118 he married Gundreda de Gourney, daughter of Gerald de Gournay and Edith, daughter of William de Warenne, Earl of Warren and Surrey and his wife Gundreda. There has been much discussion about the pedigree of this elder Gundreda. For many years she was claimed to be the daughter of William I but it is now accepted that she was the Conqueror's step daughter and a Fleming compatriot of William's wife, Matilda of Flanders.

Nigel's son, Hamon, was a Knight Templar. Following the Conquest the family had been granted lands in Leicestershire, which included Kirby Bellars, and in 1160 the estate was acquired by Hamon from his brother Roger de Molbrai, who had died in battle in 1138. Crusader "Little" Hamon took the name Belers and became Lord of Ketelby Beler. He is buried at St Mary's Church in nearby Melton Mowbray where his effigy may be seen.

Hamon's son, Samson d' Albini, assumed the alias Beller. The spelling Bellars is then taken up and passes, in turn, to Ralph, to William and to Roger, who was Sheriff of either County Leicester or Lincoln (depending on which source one believes), and thence to three Rogers in turn, to a William, a Thomas and a John and another William of Stoke d'Albini in Northamptonshire. We then pass through three Johns and to a James of Stanford (should this be Stamford?) and of Uffington in Lincolnshire, where the family put down roots for a number of generations. James was followed by his son, another James, and thus to Abel Walford Bellairs to complete the line of descent from the Norman Conquest. We have already learned that Abel Walford added the "i" to the spelling of his ancient name.

13

The Mackenzies and the Darien Adventure

Reverting back to Henry Bellairs (Henry the Great), we now explore the family of his wife, Dorothy Mackenzie.

Dorothy was the daughter of Peter Mackenzie and Mary Ennis Read. Peter Mackenzie was a younger son but his wife was an heiress and it was this which enabled them to live at Grove House, Twickenham, a large mansion now demolished. The family came to England from Jamaica where Peter's father, George Mackenzie, had extensive sugar estates and had been a Member of the Jamaican Legislative Assembly. They lived at Farenough, in Clarendon, located in the middle of the Island almost immediately north of Kingston. George's father, Alexander Mackenzie, had settled in Jamaica but not by intent, for he had participated in the mad cap Darien adventure from which he was lucky to have escaped with his life.

In the late 17th century a seventeen year old Scot called William Paterson ran away to Bristol and picked up a boat to Jamaica, there to seek his fortune. This he achieved and ten years later he went to London having learned much about trade and finance. He had never been to Darien, modern day Panama in Central America, but had heard stories about it and had acquired some charts of the area. More to the point he had developed a passion to found a Scottish colony there.

He envisaged the colony as the conduit through which trade would pass from Europe and the Atlantic to the Pacific and beyond. Initially this would be by pack horse, across the narrow isthmus, but eventually a canal would be built, thus saving thousands of miles and avoiding the treacheries of Cape Horn.

Paterson had founded the Bank of England in 1694 and it was to England that he went to raise the necessary £400,000, but he was thwarted by the East India Company which feared competition. He then tried various of the German states, but to no avail.

He eventually turned to his native Scotland for the capital, a gigantic sum for a much smaller country. There was, nevertheless, a passionate wave of national fervour and this resulted in the money being raised. In

1693 the Scottish Parliament passed an act which led to the founding of the Indian and African Company of Scotland which would give to Scotland a monopoly of Darien trade with Asia, Africa and America.

In 1698 five ships sailed from Leith with 300 gentlemen on board plus 1200 men, women and children. Each man was promised 50 acres of land and a site for a town house in the new capital, to be called New Edinburgh. They were given a rousing and patriotic send off but had only the haziest notion of where they were going. No one on board had ever been to Darien. The command structure authorised by the expedition directors was one that might have been designed not to work. A Council of ship's captains was chosen to lead the project. Neither Paterson nor any landsman was among them and no chairman was appointed. Disagreements soon developed so the Council decided to elect a chairman, but his term of office would be exactly one week, after which another would take his place! Arguments abounded. Most of the food was eaten in the first few days, but they carried a plentiful supply of goods with which to trade, including periwigs, clay pipes, hunting horns, ladies bonnets and kid gloves. One wonders if the periwigs were thought suitable for the native Indians in the swamps of Darien and the hunting horns for the Spanish colonists?

On 1 November, their navigation led them accurately to their destination, at first glance a paradise, which they named Caledonian Bay. They made peaceful contact with the native peoples, but with no one in charge they could not agree on the most basic of things. After months of wrangling, with nought but rotten food to eat, disaster struck. They had arrived at the beginning of the dry season but it was now April and it rained. With the rains came mosquitoes, with mosquitoes came malaria and with malaria came death. They died like flies. Within months a quarter had gone, and more were dying by the day. The colony had to be abandoned. Only one of the five ships, *The Caledonia*, was ever to return to Scotland, and that only after having first staggered to New York with less than a third of the crew remaining alive after a treacherous two months voyage from Darien.

News of happenings travelled slowly across the Atlantic in those days, yet on 19 September 1699 news reached Edinburgh from London of the calamity that had befallen the expedition. The directors were struck dumb and simply refused to believe it. A second fleet was about to sail to bolster the first. The captains of the waiting fleet were informed: "We are advised of a story made and propagate in England, viz., that the Scots have deserted their colony of Caledonia." The captains scoffed at this news from the dastardly English and immediately set sail. This second expedition was of four ships and 1300 men and met a similar fate to the first, except that this time the Spanish colonists also joined in the sport.

Alexander Mackenzie would have been 30 years old when he sailed for Darien. He managed to escape aboard the *St Andrew*, a ship of the first expedition. It was a perilous voyage during which she withstood a mutiny, was chased by the Spanish fleet and survived a ferocious storm which left here with torn and rotten rigging. Hardly surprising that she was unable to go to the aid of the stricken *Unicorn*. By the time she landed in Jamaica she had lost her captain and 130 men and most of those that made it to dry land died a miserable death of disease.

Alexander, however, survived to tell the tale; no doubt he found it a distinct advantage being one of the original 300 gentlemen. He found Jamaica a paradise with delicacies of every kind easily obtainable. He settled at Farenough, in Clarendon, and became a considerable land owner, no doubt managing his estates with slave labour. Here the family lived for more than 100 years, regularly sailing to England where their sons and daughters received their education, until the emancipation of the slaves brought their idyll to a close. And so to England and to Twickenham where they settled.

14

Mackenzies, Isabella of Angoulême and Charlemagne

Prior to Darien, Alexander Mackenzie's ancestors go up the line of the Mackenzies of Kintail for many generations, marrying on the way, at one time or another, Janet Linan, Isobel Cuthbert, Annabella Mackenzie of Fairburn, Helen Lovell of Balumbie, Agnes Fraser of Lovat, Anne McDougall of Dunolly, Fynvola Macleod of Harris and Isabel Macauley of Lochbroom. Sorry to relate that the author's 25 greats grandfather, one Kenneth Mackenzie, was executed in 1346, for we know not what, yet we grieve for his widow, Fynvola Macleod of Lewis, to this day. Kenneth's father, John Mackenzie of Kintail, married Margaret de Strathbogie and now we go up a number of female lines. Margaret was the daughter of the Earl of Athol and Joan Comyn. Joan was the daughter of John Comyn of Badenoch and his wife, another Joan, who was the daughter of William de Valence, Earl of Pembroke. William's parents were Hugh X de Lusignan and his wife Isabella d'Angoulême. Isabella was the widow of King John and herein lies another tale.

Shortly before her marriage to King John, Isabella, a beautiful and precocious thirteen year old, had been betrothed to Hugh de Lusignan but John was smitten by her at first sight and, despite being betrothed himself to the daughter of a Portuguese count, determined to take her for his own. Isabella and John were married by the Archbishop in Bordeaux Cathedral on 24 August 1200. But the Lusignans were a powerful and influential family, and their resentment at King John's perfidiousness was to lead

Charlemagne (courtesy of Hulton Getty Picture Collection

to the loss of great swathes of his inherited Plantagenet Empire, much of what is now western France.

John, the one really outrageous English King, so awful that Magna Carta was extracted from him, died in 1216 and is buried in Worcester Cathedral. Hugh then had his just reward by marring Isabella in the following year. Both had been born in France, Hugh in Vienne in 1183 and Isabella in Charente a year earlier and from here our story remains predominantly in France, scaling the dizzy heights of the French Royal House and eventually arriving at the door of Charlemagne.

Isabella d'Angoulême's tomb is in Fontevrault Abbey alongside those of Henry II, his Queen Eleanor of Aquitaine, and their son Richard I. Isabella was the daughter of William V Taillefer, Count Aymer of Angoulême and Alice de Courtenay. Alice was the daughter of Pierre, he the son of Louis VI of France he of Phillipe I, he of Henry I, he of Robert II, he of Hugh Capet, he of Hugh the Great and he of Earl Robert. Robert's mother was Adelaide who was the daughter of Louis I and Ermingarde, and Louis was the son of Charlemagne. Charlemagne was born on 2 April 747 and was the author's 41 greats grandfather. Other ancestors along the way include a number of exotic and distinguished ladies such as Bertha of Holland, Yaroslavna of Kiev, Hedwig of Germany and Emma Perigord. Genealogy is full of amusements!

15

Bradshaws and Isherwoods

We have learned in a previous chapter of the Herculean efforts made by Charles Bellairs to gain the hand of Anna Maria Bradshaw-Isherwood of Marple Hall in Cheshire, so who were the Bradshaws and who were the Isherwoods?

Marple is near Stockport and the original Marple Hall was built in the 1480s. Henry Bradshaw lived there as a tenant from 1590 and in 1606 purchased both Marple Hall and the more modest Wyberslegh Hall (sometimes Wybersley). In 1658 his grandson, Sir Henry Bradshaw rebuilt Marple Hall out of red sandstone. It overlooked the Goyt, a romantic stream which flows into the Mersey.

Sir Henry Bradshaw (a seven greats grandfather) was the third successive Henry to live at Marple Hall. The family was staunch Parliamentarian and, as a Colonel in Cromwell's Army, Henry was wounded at the Battle of Worcester on 16 September 1651. Not too seriously one supposes, for later the same month he was a member of the Court Martial that tried the Earl of Derby. After the Restoration he was summoned before the Lords Committee to answer for his part at Derby's trial but was treated leniently and passed his remaining days in peace. He died at Marple Hall in 1662/3.

Sir Henry Bradshaw

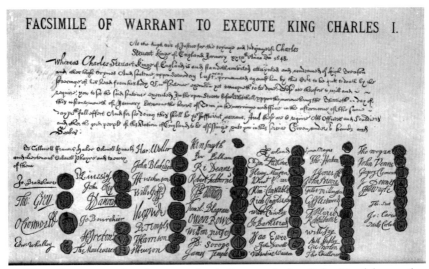

FACSIMILE OF WARRANT TO EXECUTE KING CHARLES I.

Henry's younger brother was the infamous Judge John Bradshaw who was President of the Court which tried Charles I. His was the first signature on the King's death warrant, which may be seen at the Palace of Westminster. It was signed by every member of the court so that no one could later wriggle out of responsibility for this heinous act. Cromwell was the third signatory and Ireton was well down the list. Bradshaw had his hat lined with steel plates as protection against assassination and was rewarded by being buried with honours at Westminster Abbey in 1659. After the Restoration, however, he was "hanged" at Tyburn for his pains, together with Cromwell and Ireton. A gruesome sight this must have been.

Judge Bradshaw received part of his education at Macclesfield, where, with extraordinary prescience, he inscribed on a tomb stone:

My brother Henry shall heir the land,
My brother Frank shall be at his command,
While I poor Jack, will do that,
Which all the world will wonder at.

Francis was the third son of Henry and, yes, 350 years later the world is still wondering at that.

Marple was every inch a puritan house. The windows contained German glass representing biblical subjects and the dining room was dimly lit by one small oblong window. At the time of the Civil War the muzzle loaded guns were kept by the fire place to prevent the powder becoming damp, in compliance with Cromwell's famous command: "Trust in God but keep your powder dry." The old gun racks remained at Marple until well into the 20th century.

In the hall were portraits of Katherine Wynnington, wife of the second Henry and mother of Sir Henry, Judge Bradshaw and Francis, and also one of Milton, who was Cromwell's Latin Secretary and possibly a cousin. Cromwell stayed at Marple at least once and would have been pleased on seeing the engraving of the plan of Naseby where the final defeat of the Royalists took place. Marple was haunted, for the figure of Charles I was often to be seen striding along the terrace - his head neatly tucked under his arm.

Judge John Bradshaw.

Sir Henry's son, another Henry, had two sons and a daughter, another Henry, Thomas and Mary. Neither son had issue. Mary married William Pimlott, and on being widowed married secondly Nathaniel Isherwood, the felt maker from Bolton mentioned in an earlier chapter. Thus the Bradshaw-Isherwoods. Mary and Nathaniel had two sons, Nathaniel and Thomas. Nathaniel married Elizabeth Brabyns and had no issue. Thomas had a son John, the squire who was to find Charles Bellairs such a suitable suitor for his daughter, Anna-Maria.

The 20th century was a sad one for Marple Hall. It suffered the fate of so many houses not generally lived in. The then absentee owner was Henry Bradshaw-Isherwood-Bagshaw. Henry could not resist adding his wife's name to his own to give the triple surname. His younger brother Frank and his wife Kathleen (née Machell-Smith) lived at nearby Wyberslegh Hall or in London but all the while Marple Hall steadily deteriorated. In 1929 the furniture was sold at auction. Frank Isherwood was a Lt. Col. and was killed in the First World War and so on Henry's death, childless in 1940, Frank's elder son, the author Christopher Isherwood, inherited the estates, including both Marple and Wyberslegh Halls.

Christopher Isherwood was living in California by then and had a disdain for tradition. He immediately declared that he would pass Marple on to his younger brother Richard, though the formal deed of gift could not be signed until 1947 due to the war. Christopher's diary shows that he followed the war news closely, recording the blitz on London with concern and the beginnings of the Battle of Britain. In July 1940 Richard and Kathleen left London and returned to the safety of Wyberslegh Hall.

Christopher Isherwood lived in Santa Monica throughout his 50 years in America and in 1999, Don Bacardy, his executor and companion for more than 30 years, arranged for his literary archive to be deposited. Fighting for possession were the New York Public Library, the University of Texas, UCLA and USC, but it was the Huntington Library in Los Angeles that he chose. An elated *Los Angeles Times* enthused: "The collection will comprise a unique contemporaneous literary and visual record of an extraordinarily broad and influential artistic circle." Writer Joan Didion, a lifelong friend, described Isherwood as "the strongest voice among European emigrés who forever changed the culture of Los Angeles, took it into the world and made it the least provincial of American cities."

Richard Isherwood loved Marple Hall but was quite incapable of managing it and it was just a question of time before its condition gave cause for concern. He was intelligent and knowledgeable yet he lived his life as if in a dream. He was impractical and thoroughly disorganised. He had a good memory and would flash out the answers on *Mastermind* and *Brain of Britain*. He was proud of Christopher and to a degree rather basked in his reflected light. The brothers corresponded regularly between Wyberslegh and California. Richard always sent Christopher a "cablegram," as he called it, on his birthday. He had a generous nature, describing my parents as "staunch friends." He was Godfather to my brother, Humphrey, who was very pleased to have been left a nominal £100 in Richard's will.

In 1950, with the house in a sorry state, the last caretaker left Marple Hall and within hours part of the roof collapsed and the chimney stack and clock tower crashed through to the hall. Christopher visited Richard in 1956 and saw Marple Hall for the last time. In 1958 Richard told my father that the interior was "a complete shambles" and that "there was not a pane of glass in the place." The death knell came shortly afterwards. Marple Urban District Council took over the property with a view to preserving it as a ruin but even that modest aspiration could not be achieved and Marple Hall was demolished in 1959. Only the foundations mark the spot today. A school was later built on the estate.

My first visit to Marple Hall was as a three year old, but I would have known nothing about it had it not been for Richard asking me to sign the visitors book when I visited him at his bungalow, which he had built alongside Wyberslegh Hall, in 1973. He referred back and discovered that this was the precise anniversary of my visit in August 1942. I have since found photographs of my parents on that visit but neither my brother nor I were considered worthy of inclusion. I am told that, to much amusement, I called Kathleen "Mrs Wishywood." She let me play with Christopher's old teddy bear, until, that is, I started to pull it apart when it was gently taken away from me. During our 1973 visit Richard gave us a tour of Wyberslegh Hall and a sad state it was in, with what I am sure were once fine books rotting on the shelves. Any suggestion that perhaps we should dry them out and tidy the place up was met with a wringing of hands in anguish and sighs of despair.

Richard's father, Frank, had been a professional soldier. He had served in the Boer War and was killed at Ypres in May 1915. He was a Colonel in the York and Lancaster Regiment but his body was never found. He was reported missing and one can only imagine the anguish through which Kathleen lived during those awful months of hope and despair, not knowing whether her husband was dead or alive. Fellow officers contacted hospitals and casualty stations, both at the front and at home, and the War Office was visited by friends on her behalf. Two months later Kathleen received a letter from the War Office telling her that his identity disc had been found near Frezenberg and asking her if she "would be obliged to say whether she was prepared to accept this information and begs to express on behalf of Lord Kitchener his sincere sympathy."

In August Kathleen wrote in her diary "wore black for the first time. Very depressing." On 8 September Frank's name was listed as "Previously reported missing now reported dead" and on the following day a telegram of condolence was received from the King and Queen. Kathleen's cousin, the author Graham Green, replied to the Keeper of the

Privy Purse on her behalf: "Please convey to Their Majesties with humble duty our grateful appreciation of their gracious sympathy." "I should never have dreamt of putting humble duty" wrote Kathleen in her diary!

In her last years Kathleen had visitors "quite often" and her mind remained in a perfect state. Richard would order a taxi once a week to take her shopping to Marple but its rural character was rapidly changing, Richard tells us, with "jerry-built" houses on the outskirts for the "rough-slum element from Manchester." They would have lunch at "a nice café, plain food but excellent cooking" where they would be served by "a most vigorous waitress, rather horse-like in profile with small smouldering eyes, a jutting out nose, a receding chin (not that she looks a weak character, as the chin might imply) and a turned-on smile. Except that she is decidedly clean, with a clean white apron and quite smart blouse. She is suggestive in her bearing and her expression is that of an unpleasant lavatory maid." Richard concludes: "For all I know this woman may be the essence of respectability and is always pleasant enough in what she says but her voice has a truculent "bold" note." Kathleen's observations are not recorded.

Kathleen was a widow for 45 years and died at Wyberslegh in 1960 aged 91. At her request Richard scattered Kathleen's ashes under a tree in the front garden of Wyberslegh Hall, as his were to be scattered nineteen years later. Wyberslegh then passed to a cousin on Richard's death. It was sold at auction in 1988, one hopes not to a property speculator more interested in the land development value than in restoring an historic house, and a listed one at that. Currently the structure is in a pitiful state, only the shell of the building remaining in tact and the garden is totally overgrown. One hopes that it is not permitted to collapse, for only a miracle could save it from the same fate as its more illustrious partner, Marple Hall.

16

William Seaforth Alderson

Back to the main Alderson line, to the son of George Henry William Alderson and Laura Bellairs.

I only wish I had known my grandfather, William Seaforth Alderson, but he died ten years before I was born. He was the third of the four brothers born in Canada, on 3 April 1878 at Port Rowan on Lake Erie. When William was a year old the family moved to near Little Current on Manitoulin Island in Lake Huron.

My grandfather and his brothers loved Windybush, the brave befriended by their father, who would tell them stories about his Indian way of life. They never forgot his kindnesses and the forest lore he taught them about fishing or shooting the rapids in canoes.

In later years William told my father that he played with Indian boys and that they would take him with them to pick wild raspberries and play their traditional games. They lived at Alderson's Point and when I visited there in 1994 I learned that where my grandfather had lived is still alongside the Indian Reserve and that the wild raspberries still grow there. Alderson's Point might now be White's Point but the old name was still recognised by local residents, though it was also referred to as "Bug Island!"

My grandmother, Julia Alderson (née Bland), lived to be 100. She was born in Bradford on 21 September 1867 and was an intelligent and determined lady. She became a "Certificated" school mistress under Forster's reforming Education Act and, at the age of 22, secured an appointment as Headmistress at Brimington, near Chesterfield in Derbyshire.

The music teacher at Brimington was a nephew of Guillaume, the organist of Notre Dame in Paris, and it was through him that Julia met and was befriended by an old gentleman. He took her out in his "tub-gig" to such places as Bolsover Castle. The old gentleman was George Henry William Alderson and his son, William, was learning the violin. William and Julia were married at Shipley Parish Church on 23 December 1899. William was aged 21 and Julia 32.

Wedding congratulations were received on 30 December from Uncle

Frank Alderson of Welsh Frankton. Writing from Gannow he enclosed "a small cheque as a wedding present from your Aunt and I." He reported on the appaling weather, frost, snow and gales and on "the terrible war we are having; no doubt the strength of the Boers was estimated as far too low but they must be crushed or we shall loose South Africa entirely." He then goes on to lament "the many brave fellows being cut down, many of them whilst mere boys..." and yet "I am the son of an officer yet never had the smallest wish to join the army... it would be worse still to kill one's fellow men."

William grew up into a tall and handsome man, six feet six inches tall by one account, and in later life 22 stone. He was said to have been a jolly man and of a kindly disposition. He was not destined to become a great musician but he enjoyed "bending his shackle," a term probably derived from the dialect word shacklebone meaning wristbone (Wright's *Dialect Dictionary*). In later life he played with Mr Walton who worked in the Bradford Taxation Office and Dr Sam Dobie, the cellist from Keighley. Haydn was the composer they enjoyed most.

William Seaforth Alderson

William had a governess as a boy, a Mrs Jephson, whom many years later he was to visit with my grandmother, at Chesterfield Almshouses. He was registered by the General Medical Council on 15 November 1907, one suspects via Leeds Medical School, whilst living at 3 Avenue Crescent, Harehills Avenue, Leeds. Shortly afterwards he became assistant to a Dr Lambert at Farsley, midway between Leeds and Bradford. Most of Farsley is now in Leeds, but they lived at Woodhall Terrace, Old Road, which is now the first road within the boundaries of Bradford.

It was at Farsley in 1909, when Julia was 41 years old, that Frank George Seaforth Alderson, my father, was born (an earlier daughter had died young). He was thus the only son of any of the four boys born in Canada who was to pass on the Alderson name.

Julia Bland

The following year the family moved to Silsden where William bought a practice from a distant cousin, a Dr Bradshaw, at 49 Skipton Road. This was to be their home until William's death in 1929.

Silsden is in a transverse valley that runs between Keighley in Airedale and Ilkley in Wharfedale. It is a small mill town near Rombold's Moor, on the edge of the great industrial belt of the West Riding. The Leeds and Liverpool Canal passes through Silsden, and the railway, from Lancashire to Bradford and Leeds is a mile or so away at Steeton.

The family enjoyed outings in their spartan Model T Ford car, which if the hood was up, did not have enough power in top gear to drive against the wind. Julia treasured any little thing with an historical connection and gave my father his delight in history. Their visits were usually directed towards monasteries and churches. A favourite on their itinerary was the chapel in Tadcaster which is the oldest dissenting edifice in England. William found all this rather tedious and on one occasion blurted out "I suppose we shall be starting on the jails next."

William was appointed Medical Referee for the Prudential Assurance Company for Silsden, and other appointments picked up along the way included attending the staff of the Midland Railway at Steeton and Silsden station, Medical Officer to the Poor-Law Union and Police

Surgeon. He later became a sidesman at Silsden Church and a member of the Parochial Church Council. Canon Peters and his family were close friends.

William was a Lieutenant in the Royal Army Medical Corps during the earlier part of the First World War, serving in Salonika. The degree to which he was involved is uncertain but he certainly took the opportunity to visit Athens and be photographed in front of the great temples. In April 1917, however, we find him back in Silsden and corresponding with a senior consultant in Leeds about a medical diagnosis.

In October 1918 William was rated Grade 3 following a medical examination at Halifax by the National Service Medical Board. I have a hazy recollection of my Grandmother referring to the hot days and cold nights of Salonika disagreeing with her husband, which ever afterwards affecting his bronchitis. It is likely that he was invalided out before the armistice.

William died in 1929 aged 51. The windows at 49 Silsden Road had to be removed to get the coffin out of the house. Large numbers lined the streets as the cortege travelled the short distance to the packed church. The Rev. Peters, in conducting the funeral service, referred to William as "always maintaining the highest traditions of a great and honourable profession, a devout Christian who was always present when his medical duties allowed him to come to church, a man of untiring kindness and self-sacrificing generosity."

17

Julia and the Blands

William's widow, my grandmother Julia, née Bland, was a very positive and assertive lady and was the driving force behind the family, constantly urging William forward. She was bold and upright, honest and true, and despite being ten years older than her husband was to outlive him by 38 years. Many were in awe of her and my mother always referred to her as Madam, a term of address which suited the temperament of both of them. To my brother and me, however, she was Grannie Alderson and we were very fond of her. She had a sense of fun, despite her years, for she was in her 80s when we were small boys. She would buy us Biggles' books for our birthdays and I am pleased that I still have a number of them inscribed in her confident Victorian hand "with Grannie's dearest love."

Julia was proud of her age and her catch phrase was "I'm 83," or "I'm 84," and so on as the years rolled by. The war years necessitated thrift and she would make her own handkerchiefs from scraps of material which she called "snitchers." She would put things in a safe place and then forget where the safe place was, but she would always laugh about this as we searched the house for the missing goods.

Julia was the eldest child of John Bland and Emily Burrow and was followed into the world by John, Henrietta, twins Louis and Florry and George. All the girls lived to a good age but Julia was the only one to marry. John went prospecting for oil in Ohio and is believed to have descendants there to this day but contact has been lost. George went to Bingley Grammar School and became North Eastern Manager for Joseph Rank's Flour Mills. Twins Louis and Florry opened a school near Roundhay Park in Leeds, partly financed by my grandfather, and in later life retired to a residential home in Ipswich.

On one occasion my mother took Humphrey and me to visit Florry, (Louis had died by then) the only time I remember meeting any of them. Strange that my father, who was always interested in the family and its history and who had a car and liked a drive, had little or no contact with relatives. The journey from Hull to Ipswich was, however, a substantial

John Bland

one in those days. Julia travelled around the Bradford area on a safety bicycle. She saw the Shah of Persia on his visit to the City in July 1889 and later was shown into the audience chamber where she noticed black marks on the wall where his entourage had leaned their heads. On a more sombre note, she was shown the spot, behind Bradford Town Hall, where her great uncle was garroted - or so it is said - by a ruffian who stole his watch and false teeth which were set in a matrix of gold!

Julia grew up at the Bland family farmhouse in Town Lane, Idle. The farm land was then let, but prior to the late 18th century the Blands had farmed there and Julia's father, John, had been born there.

My grandmother remembered playing in the barn loft as a little girl, and with the old farm implements, the dog cart and the horse. This, or the trips to Morecambe, were much more fun, she said as a small girl, than to see the "tinthemiz." Whatever could she mean? After much puzzlement and several attempts to draw it out of her, it appeared that she had remembered the vicar saying "tinthemiz" during his sermon in church, which, when decoded, translated into "all that in there is."

My grandmother is said to have been given a pair of finger bowls by the Peel family, their last mention in this story, but they were of inferior quality and she was not impressed.

The Blands had thrown in their lot with the Hargreaves, the last of whom, George Hargreaves, was the brother of John's mother. George had fallen out with the Church of England, as had many manufacturers at that time, and he gave most of the money to build the Chapel at Windhill. According to my father, at the meeting convened to launch the project, "the vulgar old ruffian" threw a handful of sovereigns onto the floor saying "spend that and then come back for more!"

Hargreaves prospered and in 1820 built Providence Mill at Shipley, a very large worsted mill with 1400 power looms. He lived at Shipley Fields House, later pulled down to make way for the Midland Railway. He did not marry so took his favourite nephew, John Bland, to live with him and to learn the business, intending to make him his heir. He sent John to Pannal Boarding School at Low Moor, Steeton but John married for love rather than gratify the wish of his uncle, who had taken a niece called Pullen to live with him. The promised inheritance did not materialise.

John remained a worsted manufacturer and he and Emily lived at Temple Rhydding. They did not find the adjustment easy with six children to bring up, but that they managed is borne out by the educational standards that their children achieved and the fulfiled lives that they all led. Photographs suggest that John was a homely man, though presumably he had an active social life, for we know that on 29 August 1853 he attended the opening of St George's Hall in Bradford.

Julia outlived my father and ended her days peacefully in a nursing home at Beverley. She celebrated her 100th birthday with a glass of sherry on 21 September 1967 and died a month later on 27 October. She is buried in the family grave at Silsden.

18

The Canadian Brothers and Aunt Annie Keatinge

With four healthy sons George Henry William and Emily Alderson might have been forgiven for thinking that the Alderson name was secure in this line but it was to be a close run thing, and indeed remains so today, for my brother's thirteen year old son, Christopher William Bellairs Alderson, is the only one of the younger generation able to carry it forward. So what became of William's Canadian brothers, Francis, Charles and George Ennis Christopher?

The eldest was Francis Bellairs, or Frank. He trained to became a doctor in Sheffield and in 1899 we find him writing to Aunt May, wife of his uncle, Rev Frank Alderson of Welsh Frankton in Shropshire, thanking her for a food parcel which included a big pork pie. "It was delicious" writes Frank, "I had a few friends in on Thursday and the general verdict was that the pie was a credit to the person who made it." Frank expresses regret that Aunt May's new horse had turned out to be so awkward, particularly as Uncle Frank had been so fortunate with his horses up until then.

Frank goes on to explain that the doctor he is under visits the wards on Sunday mornings, so he can only get away on alternate Sundays. Tragically he died of diphtheria within a week of qualifying. He was courting a girl in Sheffield at the time and she never recovered from the loss of her fiancé.

Charles Henry, the second son, married Rosa but they had no children. He died in 1964 aged 87, having outlived his wife by ten years. He had been a surveyor, was a Chartered Member of the Institute of Auctioneers and had at one time worked at Somerset House. He advocated the diligent teaching of the commandments and complained that "a community of atheists dominates."

Charles was the only one of the four brothers that I met. I was eleven and my mother took Humphrey and me to London to see the great Festival of Britain in 1951. This was a long journey from Yorkshire in those days and a real adventure. Uncle Charles lived in Battersea and we called to see him on the way to the Festival Fun Fair in Battersea Park.

His wife Rosa had only one leg but she was very sweet. Charles was friendly and clearly pleased to see us and he and Mother talked animatedly for more than an hour. Shortly before we left, great uncle Charles was standing in front of the fire place with his hands behind his back and we heard a distinct clinking sound. This could be only one thing and, sure enough, out popped half a crown for each of us.

Charles was the last Alderson to derive income from the Ulley lands in South Yorkshire, the final part of an estate that had been in Alderson hands for many years. No doubt he appreciated the £50 per year which he drew from the Stavely Iron and Coal Company for the first option on the mineral rights. Charles was not a wealthy man; Julia, brother William's wife, who had driven first her husband, and then her son, ever forward, considered him to have wasted his opportunities, something she could not easily forgive.

The youngest son, George Ennis Christopher Alderson, married Kate Tobin at Pontefract in 1899 and they had a son and two daughters, Christopher, Mary and Frances, known as Kit, Mayflower and Seaforth, all born between 1900 and 1904. Their father, also called Kit, was described by my father as "a kind, gentle and good looking man but struck down with Rheumatic VDH when in his forties." Seaforth described her father as "a dreamy impractical man who disappeared from our lives in his early twenties when Mother died giving birth to me prematurely. We never heard from him again." Later evidence suggests that in 1908 he married again at Ashton-under-Lyne in Lancashire. Kate Tobin had died before my father was born, yet he was able to describe her, presumably from what his father had told him, as "an Irish girl, quick and intelligent with fire in her eyes and movements, very like the famous portrait of Caroline Lamb, Countess Melbourne, the one with short hair like a page and wearing a page's costume." Kate is said to have been related to Judge Tobin, distinguished in the history of criminal jurisprudence. She is buried in the Roman Catholic cemetery in Leeds.

Following the death of their mother it was decided that Mayflower and Seaforth should live with their twice widowed yet childless great aunt, Annie Keatinge, who formally adopted them. Aunt Annie was the youngest sister of their grandfather, George Henry William Alderson, she who had been born just a month before the death of Jonathan, her father, in 1850. What a contrast this was to be. Away from the factory chimneys and industrial grime of the North of England to leafy Sussex by the

Seaforth, Tiger Gordon and Mayflower climbing trees at Lynwood.

sea and the small town of Horsham. Aunt Annie had married one Edward Charlton Fox but had been widowed. She married secondly General Richard Harte Keatinge, VC, CSI, himself a widower.

Keatinge had had a distinguished Army career. He joined the Bombay Artillery in 1842 and served through the Indian Mutiny. He received the Victoria Cross at the siege of Chandari where he led the column through the breach and was dangerously wounded. His horse was shot from under him during three days of fighting at Mundesor. He became the Governor General's agent in the Rajputana States in 1867, Governor of the North West Provinces and Chief Commissioner of the Central Provinces in 1870 and of Assam from 1873 to 1880. Keatinge was a director of the Bombay and Aroda Central India Railway. He was award-ed the Companion of the Order of the Star of India (CSI). He was later appointed military attaché to the Tsar and, with Aunt Annie, lived in St Petersburg. He died in May 1904 and is buried at Horsham Cemetery.

The arrival of the two adopted girls, and within a month or so of the death of the General, must have caused quite a stir at Lynwood, Aunt Annie's Horsham home. Seaforth tells us "it was a great shock to the household when the Great Aunt," as Seaforth called her, "returned one day in the brougham with two babies." Nurse Reeves was quickly appointed. There is no mention of Kit, who would have been four when his mother died. Perhaps he stayed with his father but he certainly visited Horsham for holidays for he is included in many of the family photographs taken at Lynwood.

Lynwood was probably a late Georgian house with numerous rooms, many only used when visitors came to stay, often for months on end. There was a stable and yard, an outside laundry and a lovely large garden containing a huge mulberry tree, peach trees and a yew. In summer the wisteria threw scented lilac plumes and pale green coils of tendrils in at the open windows. In a sad corner of the garden was an old cottage where the chickens perched, the goats played and an old vine produced sour little grapes.

Aunt Annie was modern in outlook. She was trained at the Slade School of Art in London yet had mechanical as well as artistic talents. Like her brother George, she was an excellent wood carver and also an accomplished painter and jewel setter. She designed a fine mosaic for the headstone of her husband's tomb in Horsham cemetery, embracing the Keatinge coat of arms, which she laid out with her own hands. She had an electric cooker as early as 1914 which was heated by carbon filament lamps, and long before anyone else thought of it she had central heating installed with aluminium painted radiators.

Her first car was a Steam car. She then bought a Napier, which she decarbonised herself and then taught the chauffeur how to

Aunt Annie Keatinge

drive it. She later had a Daimler. She was a prolific correspondent, writing five or more letters a day. She was offered a grace and favour apartment at Hampton Court when the General died but declined it.

From Seaforth we learn that the Great Aunt had very large diamond earrings, bracelets and necklaces made of diamonds, sapphires and emeralds and that she wore them always. "They suited her; it was timeless and always fashionable." She believed it important to go to church to set a good example and sit in the family pew in the front row, but "we must never, never believe a word the parson said" she told the girls. She was a fervent spiritualist and really believed in the after-life and the unimportance of death. Her beliefs made her serene and happy and she longed for everyone else to share her joy. Years later, her nephew Charles was to write, that "Aunt Annie knew many things but she failed to realise that God is truth."

Every week Aunt Annie would have all the chamber pots lined up in one of the spare bedrooms. She would then give each in turn a sharp tap with a poker to see if it rang true. It appears that some years earlier a niece, who was being married from the house, had cut herself badly on a cracked chamber pot on the night before her wedding, necessitating her wedding having to be postponed for a fortnight. Explanations had proved difficult.

The Great Aunt was a good shot both with an air-gun and with bow and arrow. One day a smart car drew up with a coronet imprinted on the door and with two men in chauffeurs' uniforms in the front. An elegant French woman asked to see "the lady of the house." Her mistress, a Russian Princess, wished to rent the house for the season. This coincided with an invitation to the Great Aunt to compete for the Ladies Archery Team with France at Le Touquet. Negotiations were carried out between the children's governess and the French lady and terms agreed. So, leaving things in the hands of the governess, the gardener and the housekeeper, the Great Aunt, never having stayed away from Lynwood since first moving there, went to France without ever seeing the mysterious Princess.

On their return the housekeeper, Mrs Wood, who had neither approved of letting the house to the Princess nor of Aunt Annie departing for France, duly reported. The Princess, it transpired, was half Greek and was very rich, very fat, wore a wig and walked about upstairs naked. Her valet bathed her. She ate copious amounts of ham fat, toffee and cream cakes. She was ostentatious and had a priceless collection of jewellery. On one occasion she had it displayed on a large table and from it flung a watch at Fuller, the chauffeur, cutting his face. This was a gift and was her way of thanking him.

My father looked forward to his boyhood holidays at Horsham with his great aunt and cousins during the years of the Great War. Aunt Annie Keatinge was 60 years his senior yet he loved to listen to her talk and remembered many things that she taught him; how to sharpen a pencil with a chisel, for example, or how to protect his hands from onion smells after he had helped to peel them. He records that there were some who would mock him because of his northern short "a" but not Aunt Annie who told the assembled presence that "when I first went to Court there were many who used the short "a" and we all kept to our own style" - and to Frank "do not let anyone put you off yours." Yet I do not remember Frank's short "a" so perhaps Aunt Annie's advice was forsaken for once.

Frank spent the lazy days of summer playing on the swing with his cousins, Mayflower and Seaforth, and with Tiger Gordon, General Gordon's niece, who was a regular visitor to Lynwood. They enjoyed climbing trees and playing carefree games in the lovely large garden. Frank would collect the tea leaves for gardener Leadbeater's roses.

Frank was taken to a Guide Jamboree and was polite when introduced to the Baden-Powells. He loved to hear the stories of Prince Ranjitsinghi, the great Indian cricketer, who often stayed at Lynwood when playing for Sussex.

Mayflower and Seaforth's brother, Christopher, a fine looking boy judging by photographs, died of disease in South Africa in 1924, on an ox-cart, it is said, as medical treatment was being sought. He was 24 years old and was living on the Tuanda Tea Estate at Verulam near Durban. One doubts that the recently departed Gandhi was his role model, for a later photograph shows him as a big game hunter, supporting himself with a rifle in each hand, a revolver tucked under his belt, ammunition belt slung over his shoulder, white shorts, knee high leggings, pith helmet, neckerchief and cigar dangling from his lips; every inch the white man about the South African bush. His untimely death left my father, then sixteen, as the only remaining male Alderson in this line, with the exception of his 48 year old Uncle Charles.

Aunt Annie died in the great influenza epidemic that struck shortly after the end of the Great War, that which took more lives than were lost in the war itself. Mayflower and Seaforth were then made Wards of Court. Seaforth went to a girls boarding school in Seaford in Sussex and then to Cambridge University where she met Basil Creighton, married him, and lived happily ever afterwards.

Mayflower was sent to school in Cumberland where she was looked after by Colonel Bethune, an old friend of the Great Aunt, who promptly fell in love with her. She then had a love affair with a son of the Norfolks of Arundel but this was thought to be an unsuitable match. To help her get over this she went on holiday to South Africa with "Tiger" Gordon and on the ship coming home she met an engineer, Christopher Gordon Downie, and married him.

Christopher Downie was born in Francistown, Bechuanaland (now Botswana) in 1902, the eldest of the seven children of Christopher Gordon Downie and Margaret Barron Murray, both from Glasgow. They had emigrated to Africa in the early days of the century. Disaster struck in 1915 as Downie senior was killed in the Planet Mine near Salisbury (now Harare). Thirteen men had been trapped underground and Downie was praised for getting the other twelve to safety, all of whom were black mine workers. His widow had to be made of stern stuff with a clutch of young children to bring up single handed in the inhospitable frontier land of Africa, but she was up to the mark and saw them all into good jobs and eventual prosperity.

Christopher Downie (junior) graduated from the University of Cape Town with a 1st in Electrical Engineering and won an overseas travelling scholarship which took him to the Metropolitan-Vickers plant in Manchester. It was on the boat to England, the "Garth Castle," that he met Mayflower. They were married at Barton-upon-Irwell in Lancashire in 1924. They had two children, Mary Margaret Julia (Judy), born in Ashton-on-Mersey in 1926 and William John Gordon (Bill) born in Harrow in 1927. Familiar names again, for Julia and William were those of my grandparents, their great uncle and aunt. The family settled in South Africa where Christopher eventually become City Electrical Engineer in Cape Town.

Mayflower was described by her younger sister as being pale, mysterious and sad with large gentian blue eyes set far apart, fine black eyebrows and dark lashes. Her hair was thick and fair with a golden gleam and she had a pale brow and a reckless generosity. Her handwriting and correspondence in later life suggests a careful and rather wistful person.

Despite having lived more than half her life in Africa, Mayflower never felt it to be her home and so the couple returned to England after Christopher's retirement in 1962. They settled in Worthing at Sussex, so near to that blissful home that Aunt Annie Keatinge had made for two lost children almost 60 years earlier. She died in 1973. Her intrepid husband Christopher lived on until 1999 aged 96.

Mayflower's daughter, Judy, married Douglas Joseph Cottier from Liverpool, a Lieutenant in the Royal Air Force, and they had two sons, Christopher Edward Cottier (Chris) born in Pretoria in 1951, and Stephen William born in Chingola, Northern Rhodesia (now Zambia) in 1954. The family were unhappy with the atmosphere created by the apartheid policies of the South African government and in 1963 they moved to Shannon in Ireland for two years and then on to Canada, putting roots down in Toronto.

I met Judy Cottier just once, in London in about 1982. She made one particularly interesting observation which was that when she came to Britain for the first time since her childhood (which she was too young to remember) she was amazed to find white people doing manual work. Having heard so many stories from her mother about life at Lynwood, she had assumed that everyone lived in great mansions and had servants to look after them!

Chris Cottier, Judy's elder son, now lives in Vancouver. He married Petra Mary Dorssers, of Dutch descent, and they have two children, Douglas Gordon born in 1990 and Anna Mary in 1991. Chris regularly visited his grandfather in Sussex until his death in 1999, usually contriving to work it in with a rugby match at Twickenham, preferably with South Africa playing.

Judy's second son, Stephen, married Valerie Bochenek. They live in Toronto, close to Judy, and have children Richard Christopher and Jacqueline.

Judy's brother, Bill Downie, has remained in Cape Town. He married firstly Joyce Futeran and they have a son, Stuart, who was born in 1959. He and his family live in London. Bill's second wife was Pamela Walton and they too have a son, Kenneth, born in South Africa in 1964, where he lived until moving to New Zealand in 2000. He is a navigation officer in the merchant marine, a profession that has taken him all over the southern hemisphere.

Seaforth Alderson married Basil Creighton in 1927 and they were blissfully happy. Basil was from a family of timber merchants from Cumberland but both his parents died when he was a child and he was brought up by his uncle, the renowned Mandel Creighton, one time Bishop of Peterborough and later of London. The Bishop wrote a flow of instructive letters to his nephew, first at Uppingham and then at New College, Oxford. A career at the Bar was interrupted by the First World War, in which Basil served as an Infantry Lieutenant in the trenches before transferring to Intelligence. Here his duties were to take photographs whilst being flown over German lines.

It is primarily as a novelist and poet that Basil is remembered, producing a veritable library of works between 1917 and 1988. He was the foremost translator from German - a language which he claimed he could not speak! He would read his translation straight from the German text and Seaforth would struggle to take his words down. Paintings and music were other passions; Basil attended the premier of Richard Strauss's opera *Salome* in Munich in 1905. He and Seaforth assembled a fine collection of modern works and his understanding of music aided his translation of Alma Mahler's *Gustav Mahler: Memories and Letters.*

In an addendum to the obituary to Basil Creighton in the *Daily Telegraph*, Richard Shone wrote "Basil and Frances Creighton were a completely devoted couple, sharing all interests and enthusiasms. Basil's mischievous remarks neatly contrasted with Frances's gently hilarious accounts of the events of daily life which always seemed to take her by surprise. Both were united in their solicitous affection for their friends, their scrupulous modesty, their delight - as their world narrowed to the confines of their flat in South Kensington - in the books and pictures around them. To visit them there was to experience an unforgettable atmosphere of humming serenity."

19

Frank George Seaforth Alderson and Cicely Bray

My father was born on 5 February 1909 at Woodhall Terrace, Old Road, Farsley, midway between Leeds and Bradford. His mother, Julia, was 41 years old and Frank was an only child. He was named after his great uncle, the Rev. Frank, George after both his grandfathers and Seaforth after his father and the Seaforth-Mackenzies of Kintail; thus Frank George Seaforth Alderson. When he was very young the family moved to Silsden in Yorkshire where his father, William Seaforth, took up private practice as a doctor.

As a boy Frank liked playing on the weighing scales in the parcels room at Silsden and Steeton Station. Mr Evans, the station master, was a kindly man who explained that his hens did not need fencing in because they were born on the side of the railway and always knew when a train was coming. Joe Sommerscales was a porter who also entertained my father. One of his jobs was to light the gas lamps. He did this by walking along the tops of the lovely clerestory roofs of the coaches to reach the lamps. One Saturday evening he jumped from one coach to the next, but it was not there and he crashed onto the railway line breaking both his legs. He lost his job and Frank's father had much difficulty in getting him re-instated.

The moors were Frank's play ground. He knew every nook and cranny and I am certain that it was his love of the dry stone walls, the heather, the crags, the grouse and the tarns that persuaded him to send me to boarding school at Ilkley, despite us then living at far-away Hull. Being a Yorkshireman, it was natural to like cricket and Frank went to the Park Avenue ground in Bradford to see Yorkshire play. No doubt he saw his cousin Rockley Wilson weave his magic with the ball and certainly Wilfred Rhodes, Roy Kilner, George Macauley, Herbert Sutcliffe, Percy Holmes and a host more. He went with the Peters children from the Vicarage. They were given the bus fare for one way only, so either they walked the fourteen miles to Bradford across the moors, skirting north of Keighley, or walked the fourteen miles home.

Frank was sent to Col. Godfrey's preparatory school, Ghyll Royd, in

Frank G. S. Alderson

Ilkley, and then on to Rossall, where he was placed in Pelican House. He appears to have enjoyed school. He obtained his School Certificate in July 1925 and joined the Officer Training Corps - Junior Division - obtaining his Certificate A in March 1926.

That same year Frank went up to Pembroke College, Cambridge. He took out life membership of the Cambridge Union and paid seven and a half guineas to join the University Medical Society. He took General Biology for three terms at the Medical School, and achieved a satisfactory level, but in 1927 he left Cambridge. One suspects this was for financial reasons. In December 1926 he had sent a rather terse post card home asking his father for a further £3.

In 1927 Articles of Clerkship were drawn up, which would have bound Frank to Marmaduke Redmayne Knowles, solicitor, but they were not signed and nothing came of it.

Frank then reverted to the study of medicine for in March 1928 he passed the preliminary examination of the Royal College of Physicians and enrolled as a medical student at the University of Leeds. Six years later, in August 1934, he qualified and was awarded his LMSSA Lond. He was given glowing testimonials by senior consultants under whom he had studied and shortly afterwards commenced work with Dr Hartley at Castleford, who was said to be modern in his treatment.

Harry Clegg was a fellow student with Frank and describes him as orthodox. He always wore a plain white shirt and dark tie and usually a dark suit. He had very conservative views and was particular about correct speech. The two of them would occasionally go out for lunch if they were in town as "the medical and university food was atrocious and Frank always ordered a standard soup, beef and some sweet such as apple pie."

From his early days Frank had been attracted by mechanical things; cars, motorbikes and steam power and he and Harry Clegg had a number of student scrapes together. On one occasion Frank offered to take Harry on his Rudge motor cycle, a fast and rather swanky machine for those days, to Headingley, where Harry was playing rugger for the medics. When they were due to leave the rear tyre was flat and they did not have a pump. They searched every car in sight and eventually were offered a pump by a man with an old small Talbot. It was buried under a sack of coal in the back of his car and when they tried to use it, it let more air out of the tyre than it pumped in. So they set off with the rear tyre flat and Harry perched on a rear luggage bracket clutching his rugger gear. They roared in and out of the traffic at great speed, and sailed through the college gate and straight over a six inch step which shot poor Harry up into the air. Fortunately he landed more or less back onto the motor cycle and was just in time to play in the second half of the game.

One summer Frank decided to slim a little and started riding a bicycle in the country. Noticing no apparent change in his girth Harry asked how the campaign was going. "Not so well" said Frank "because I get so hot and thirsty that I have to keep stopping at a pub for a drink." When asked how many miles to the gallon he said "about two!"

In 1932 the Silsden practice was sold for £1400 and in 1935 Frank bought a practice in Hull for £3800 from a Dr MacQuarrie. This was on Holderness Road, which runs throughout the length of east Hull. After a year or so Frank and his mother moved to 15 Holderness Road as both home and surgery.

On 3 September 1938 Frank married Cicely Bray at St John's, Newland, in Hull and they honeymooned in London. Cicely was the only child of Frederick William Bray, who had died in 1933, and Ethel, née Chapman. Nine months later I was born and three months after that my parents celebrated their first wedding anniversary, listening to the wireless in the kitchen, as Neville Chamberlain announced that Britain was at war with Germany.

Frank made two attempts to join the army but he was a shade too portly and, in any event, it might have been considered more important to have him, a doctor, stay in Hull.

Wartime Hull was no sinecure. The city was badly bombed and we lived in Drypool, near Reckitt and Coleman's giant pharmaceutical factory (Reckitt's Blue, Dettol etc.), Ranks flour mill and the main docks. The Germans tried time and again to destroy the bridges over the River Hull, and thus cut off the large docks from the rest of the country. Like most people, Frank rarely talked about the horrors of the war, but years later he confided some of these experiences to his biographical notes. Here he mentioned the blitz, watching the great masts of the Archibald-Russell blazing in Victoria Dock or the fearful land mines flapping down on their parachutes, exploding at rooftop height and flattening several streets. It was his sad duty to certify people dead or insane, often his patients and sometimes personal friends, after the nightly terror. He would tell of servicemen home from leave who could not wait to get away from Hull to the safety of their units.

Our house was shattered by bomb blast several times but we mostly survived to tell the tale. My sister, Harriet, was the unlucky one. She was born in March 1940 but died of pneumonia in September the same year and is buried at Silsden with the grandfather she never knew. My mother never forgot to place flowers on her grave on her birthday. My brother, Humphrey William, was born in 1941.

Cicely
Bray

Some comment must be made about the names that we were given. I was christened Christopher Dominic Marmaduke Bellairs. This was asking for trouble and argument raged about what I should be known as, with the first three all in the running. Things came to a head when my grandmother screamed out in frustration "call him Nicademus" and Marmaduke was then quickly settled upon before any more damage could be done. I have, nevertheless, Christening presents inscribed with a C and a D. Harriet, poor soul, was named Harriet Vanessa Magdalene Bradshaw-Isherwood and my brother Humphrey William Carleon D'Albini, this latter name being derived from the Bellairs ancestral home in Normandy as mentioned earlier. Small wonder that he disowned most of these and settles for William. We were, however, in good company, for my mother christened the cat Lilly Axel Donabound Paté Abnegation, though my father rather spoiled the fun by calling her Lilly.

Frank George Seaforth Alderson

Towards the end of the war the family moved to a larger house overlooking Pearson Park (the practice remaining at Holderness Road) but not for long as a family, because in 1946 my parents separated as a prelude to divorce. Mother moved to Acaster Malbis, near York, taking Humphrey and me with her.

Frank was a conscientious and hard working doctor and was called out in the middle of the night many times. He would put his suit on over his pyjamas and set off grumbling and muttering. When he returned an hour later it had usually been for something trivial.

He supported the principles of the National Health Service which started in 1948, though he was unhappy with some aspects of it. At least it saved him having to write out invoices and keep accounts in his surgery at Holderness Road. I would be deposited in the dispensary as he attended his patients, with whom he was often very jolly, particularly if they were a butcher or a grocer, as he was the master at obtaining a pork joint or a dozen jars of jam on the black market for a few bob; post-War rationing was, of course, in full swing.

My father was a big man and had a sense of the ridiculous. He would read Dickens, a love he inherited from his father, who bequeathed him a full set of Dickens paperbacks published in the first decade of the 20th century. He took *Punch* and as a small boy I would climb into bed with him as he showed me the cartoons. He liked the music hall, then on its last legs, and helped it on its way by purchasing a television in time for the Queen's Coronation in 1953.

Frank had always been attracted by motor-bikes and fine cars, at various times having MG sports cars, a Jaguar, an Alvis, an Armstrong Siddeley and pre-war Rolls Royces, usually second hand but all very much quality cars. He enjoyed a drive on a Thursday afternoon, his half day off, and liked to visit old churches or go to the races. In April 1949 he backed Nimbus and Jester King in the Tote Double at Thirsk and won £112, a very large sum then, and with his winnings, bought a new Axminster carpet for the drawing room. In 1950, he took me to Headingley to see Yorkshire play Northamptonshire. This was, I believe, my first visit to a first class cricket match, for which I still have the score card.

Late in 1953 Frank had the first of a series of heart attacks and was whipped into Hull Royal Infirmary. The lease on Pearson Park was about to expire, so rather than renew it he let it lapse. A daily maid who had worked for him for some years offered to remove his furniture to safe keeping, so safe that a host of fine pieces were never seen again including two Georgian grandfather clocks. The practice in Hull was taken over by his partner Dr Keys.

When he recovered, Frank was lucky to obtain a position as assistant to a Dr Marr, the perfect partner, who practised on the Yorkshire Wolds. He moved, with his mother, to a bungalow in Wetwang, near Driffield, and bought a Morris Minor which, much to his surprise, he thoroughly enjoyed. He visited patients in Fimber, Fridaythorpe, Kirby Grindalythe, Weaverthorpe, Birdsall, Warter, Wharram-le-Street, Tibthorpe and Thixendale, driving along the narrow lanes and up and down the steep chalk hills of unspoilt East Yorkshire. Among his patients was Sir Richard Sykes of Sledmere House, but Frank found him a fusspot and rather tiresome.

The good life was not to last, however, for in late 1954 Frank was laid low again. He then moved into a 19th century semi-detached cottage, the last remaining building in the lost village of Wharram Percy, the only other inhabitants being a family of farm hands who lived next door.

Frank had discovered Wharram Percy some years earlier. It is located a mile off the main road at Wharram-le-street and he was attracted by the seclusion and the romanticism of the place. The church, partly Saxon, was dangerous and without a roof by now, and Frank rescued the Bible not long before the tower collapsed. Over a long period English Heritage has undertaken a series of summer archaeological digs at Wharram, commencing in 1950. This has shown that it was not the Black Death, as had previously been taken for granted, that had led to the village becoming depopulated, but rather the expansion of the cloth trade in the mid 16th century. This led to a sparse population of shepherds replacing a considerably larger number of ploughmen.

A 9th century Saxon cross has been discovered and also the sites of Roman villas and fragments of pottery dating from the Roman and Iron Age periods. Wharram has led to the discovery of the history of rural Britain, over a 1500 year period, and is considered the most important archaeological site of any period, anywhere in the country. Frank loved all this, as did his mother, Julia.

Presumably the winters were difficult at Wharram and in 1955 Frank moved again, this time to a cottage, which he named Gannow Cottage, in Leavening, another East Riding village. Again his mother was with him but Julia was now approaching 90 and in poor health as well as being deaf and almost blind. It must have been a relief to Frank when he found her a place in a nursing home at Gilberdyke where she was properly looked after.

In the spring of 1957 Frank made his last move, to the Tower Nursing Home at Mundesley, on the north Norfolk coast. This was the first time he had lived outside Yorkshire and he had been helped in finding it by Cicely and her second husband Michael Robson.

In August 1958 he decided to visit his beloved Wharfedale, but it turned out to be too much for him. He suffered a fatal heart attack whilst visiting Bolton Abbey, where his great grandfather, Charles Bellairs, had been rector. He is buried at Silsden, alongside his father and his daughter Harriet. He was 49.

When my parents separated Cicely moved to Acaster Malbis, a scattered village five miles from York. There she rented a large ten bedroomed house called The Manor, not an old manor house, for it was built by the Raimes family in around 1910, though it may have been on the site of something more genuine. It was a glorious place for two small boys to grow up in, with large grounds containing a ruined church that had been transposed from York that we called the Abbey! There was a lake complete with punt, generous woodland, nuttery and kitchen garden. My childhood memories are of the outdoor life, charging about on bikes, climbing trees, lighting bonfires and playing both on, and in, the lake!

I am not sure that I would regard my Mother as a great business woman but she immediately set about opening the Manor School, for day children and boarders, boys and girls. The school colours were pink and purple. Next she opened a dress making business that she called Blue Heron, for which she acquired premises at 5 Skeldergate, York, though the sewing was all done at The Manor. She advertised in *Vogue* and was inundated with work. Clients might order a wardrobe of ten or more outfits for the season. Her most esteemed customer was the Princess Royal of Harewood House, near Leeds.

Having so much land Cicely then set to work to make it pay for itself. A chicken farm was the first, followed by a piggery and, in season, she would set us on picking the thousands of beautiful daffodils and narcissi that adorned the banks of the lake, which she would sell to various shops in York.

My mother loved the stage. At one time she was a member of Hull Repertory Company and played alongside Stewart Grainger. At Acaster Malbis there was an RAF camp up the road, full of bored-to-death post war National Servicemen. To bide their time the play was the thing, and

The Manor, Acaster Malbis, York.

from the village they sought ladies for the female parts. My mother obliged and met Michael Robson, shortly to be an undergraduate at Oxford. They were married and Zulieka Rosalind Miranda Robson was born in 1953, on 29 May to be exact, the same day that Tensing and Hillary became the first to conquer Everest. After Michael's graduation they moved to Norfolk and there Jake Bartholomew Julian Ludovic Robson was born. They are Zeddie and Jake to the rest of us.

My Mother took Blue Heron with her to Norfolk but it soon fizzled out. She then opened a language school for foreign students, followed by a restaurant with a Chinese partner, a marriage bureau and, having been to Cyprus on holiday where she met Archbishop Makarios, became the British representative of the Cypriot Tourist Office – or so she claimed.

Cicely's last move was to Kew in Surrey, otherwise west London, and here she opened another language school. She also arranged conducted tours of Britain for American tourists, though this proved rather time consuming.

Quite what prompted Cicely's interest in donkeys is unclear but she held a Donkey Fair in her home to raise money to feed the poor dears after a life's work at the sea-side. Such a huge success was this, that it became an annual event, greatly looked forward to by the donkey loving fraternity of Kew.

Though hardly a domesticated person, Cicely was an excellent knitter and would knit chunky woollens which, when added to her sewing artefacts, she would exhibit at Kew Fair. She would commandeer friends to sew and knit for her and help mount a fine display.

It will be appreciated by now that Cicely had a fertile imagination when it came to names, but charity begins at home and, disliking her name of Cicely, she first changed it to Olga. After a number of years she tired of that and the second change was to Jessica, but this time she selected the new surname of Hallsmith. She then dabbled with Desfarge for a while before finally settling on Jessica Alderson-Robson, though she was always known as Cicely to the family.

Ballet was a lifelong interest and in her latter years she enjoyed the occasional visit to Covent Garden or Saddler's Wells and also to London museums and galleries. She had travelled widely and was an avid reader all her life. She died at Kew in December 2002.

20

Into the 21st Century

This book is not about me but a few words to take us into the 21st century. I spent my working life as an engineer in the aircraft industry, first with Blackburn Aircraft Company at Brough near Hull. On D-day 1964 I married Karen Christina Sackville-Bryant, daughter of Richard Walter Hugh Sackville-Bryant and May Thelma, née Hardcastle.

We then had four years in Canada and the United States, living variously in Montreal, Atlanta and Boston. Laura Harriet Camilla was born in Montreal in 1965.

In 1968 we returned to Britain and the magic of Concorde lured us to Bristol, a city that we soon came to love and in which we have put down firm roots. I became a City Councillor in 1973 and was privileged to be Lord Mayor in 1987.

Rachel Emma Seaforth was born in 1969 and Emily Hannah Bellairs in 1978, both in Bristol. On 3 April 1993 Laura married David Boddington and they have two children, Ellis Max, born in 1995 and Mia Florence in 1997. Laura is a teacher and they live in Brighton. Rachel graduated from Hull University in South East Asian Studies and works at the British Empire and Commonwealth Museum

The author, 1947

The author and his wife.

in Bristol. Emily has also travelled and spent a year in Australia. She currently works in financial services in Bristol.

And so ends our tale, thirteen generations from the start on that windswept moor on the high Pennines. Perhaps one day Ellis and Mia will add a few chapters about further generations. I am only sorry that I shall not be around to read what they may say.

Genealogy of thirteen generations of Aldersons from Simond of Muker and Miles of Keld to the present day. Numerals refer to chapter numbers.

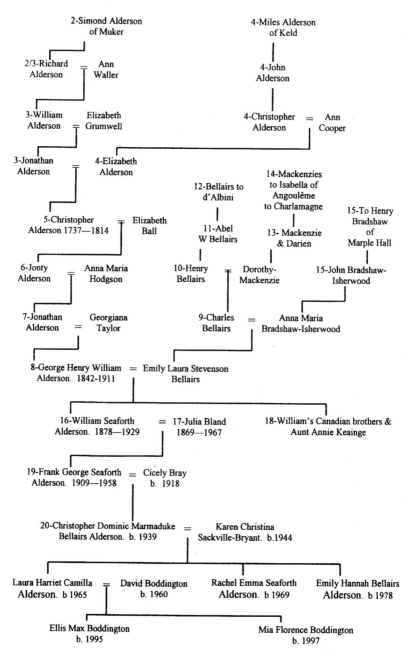

Bibliography and Sources

It is common for families to use the same Christian names down the generations and so to avoid confusion I have given every direct ancestor a unique identifier, which is in three parts: generation/sex/line. I made myself generation number 8, my parents 9, my grandparents 10 etc. Paternal or maternal ancestors are designated p or m. The linear lines are numbered numerically from left to right. Hence I am 8p1, my father and mother 9p1 and 9m1, my four grandparents 10p1, 10m1 and 10p2 and 10m2 and my eight great grandparents 11p1, 11m1, etc. to 11m8.

My computer gives every entry a serial number and the Alderson Family History Society allocates P numbers. Hence three sets of numbers are used by me or others to identify precisely to whom one is referring. I made my self generation 8, so that one simply has to delete 10 to arrive at the number of greats. Hence Gardener Alderson (14p1) is a four greats grandfather. The full identifier of my father is 9p1/9/P1001 and that of some key ancestors are quoted below.

Chapter 2 - Simond of Muker (18p1/536/P....).
Kirkby Stephen Depositions by Commission.

Chapter 3 - High Ewebank - Richard to William to Jonathan Alderson (17p1/534/P.... to 16p1/507/P2530 to 15p1/47/P1006).
The Westmorland Rentals of Lord Thanet's Estate.
The Plains of Heaven, Dawn Robertson.

Chapter 5 - Christopher "Gardener" Alderson (14p1/9/P1005).
Sedbergh School Headmaster and Archivist/Librarian.
The Church and Parish of Aston with Aughton, Yorkshire by the Reverend George Kirk.
Harleian Manuscript Familiæ Minorum Gentium MS285 - Alderson-Ball pedigree.
The Archivist of York Minster and Minster Library.
Horace Walpole Correspondence to William Mason, The Yale Edition, edited by W S Lewis.
Royal Gardens by Roy Strong.
Queen Charlotte by Olwen Hedley, pub. John Murray.

Articles from *Country Life* re. Nuneham Courtenay.

The Illustrated History of Derby Suburbs by Maxwell Craven.

JG Essame, Hon Treasurer, Oddington PCC, Gloucestershire.

Mr Stanley Grant, Warden Emeritus of Eckington, Derbyshire.

History of St Peter and St Paul Church, Eckington, Ed. by Peter Bond.

Dictionary of National Biography re. William Mason's Hull origins.

Lewis's Topographical Directory re. Brough-under-Stainmore and Eckington.

The College of Arms re. grant to Christopher and the posterity of Jonathan.

South West Yorkshire Village Book, pub by Fed of WIs 1991 re. Osborn family and Aston.

Augusta Leigh, Byron's half-sister by Michael and Melissa Bakewell.

Correspondence from Dr Jules Smith of Hull.

The Gardens of Britain by John Anthony re. Renishaw.

William Mason, Son of Hull by Gwen Staveley.

Sheffield Record Office.

Chapter 6 - Jonty Alderson and the Hodgsons (13p1/11/P1004).

Gentleman's Magazine (used extensively).

Parish of St Barnabas, Sheffield by Mary Walton, 1976, re. property in Highfield Terrace.

The Church of St Mary the Virgin, Rawmarsh with Parkgate, by Fr Roger Bellamy.

Correspondence from Fr Roger Bellamy, Rector of Rawmarsh.

A History of St Mary's Church, Rawmarsh by Phyllis M Cater.

Two Generations by Osbert Sitwell re daughters of Jonty Alderson.

Sketch of a tour to Beaumaris by Harriet Alderson.

Dr. J A R Bickford of Kirkella, near Hull and the Pease Collection at the Kingston-upon-Hull Record Office re. correspondence from Christopher Alderson, son of Gardener Alderson.

Alfred Alderson's correspondence.

Chapter 7 - Jonathan Alderson - Soldier and Farmer (12p1/14/P1003).

Association of Friends of the Waterloo Committee re. army career.

David Stanley of the Regimental Archives Research Station of the Oxfordshire and Buckinghamshire Light Infantry, Oxford.

Col. Tillett of the Royal Green Jackets Regimental Museum, Winchester.

Records of the 43rd Monmouthshire Rgt by Sir Richard Levinge.
Augusta M Alderson and Penworking AFHS NL43.
The Company of Cutlers in Hallamshire re. Wilson links.
Mike Coward and *The Australian* newspaper rc Wilson and Douglas Jardine.

Chapter 8 - George Henry William Alderson (11p1/17/P1002).
Exploring Manitoulin by Shelley J Pearen.
Unpublished biographical notes by FGS Alderson.
T J Patten writing in the Manitoulin Expositor 1932 re. The Hermitage and entertaining.

Chapter 9 - Charles Bellairs (12p2/87).
Charles Bellairs' Diary.
Kathleen and Frank by Christopher Isherwood.
Bolton Priory and its Church by Peter Watkins.
History of Sutton-in-Ashfield by Charles Bellairs.

Chapter 10 - Henry Bellairs the Great (13p3/25).
Soldier, Sailor, Priest (unpublished) by Laura P Price (née Bellairs).
The Sailing Navy List by David Lyon re the HMS Spartiate history.
Starving in Bedworth - Will Not Pay The Loan by Tony Davis.
An Appreciation of Henry Bellairs by Guy ffarington Bellairs.
The Central Library, Bristol.

Chapter 11 - Abel Walford Bellairs (14p5/64).
Stamford Museum, Lincolnshire County Council.
Rutland County Council Libraries and Museums Service.

Chapter 12 - d'Albini and Bellars.
Familia de Bellairs olim d'Albini de Albeneio in Normandiâ.

Chapter 13 - The Mackenzies and the Darien Adventure.
The Golden Isthmus by David Howarth.
Pedigree of relationship of Ennis Read to Mackenzie by Anne Maier.

Chapter 14 - The Mackenzies, Isabella of Angoulême and Charlemagne
Scots Peerage and Mackenzie Genealogies re. Lusignan pedigree.

Chapter 15 - Bradshaws and Isherwoods.
Kathleen and Frank by Christopher Isherwood.
Christopher Isherwood Diaries, Vol. I.
Los Angeles Times press reports re. Isherwood archives.
Booklet on Marple Hall, author unknown.
Correspondence from Richard Isherwood to the author.

Chapter 16 - William Seaforth Alderson (10p1/20/P1001).

Chapter 17 - Julia and the Blands.
Biographical notes compiled by FGS Alderson.

Chapter 18 - The Canadian Brothers and Aunt Annie Keatinge.
An Edwardian child in Sussex by Seaforth Creighton, née Alderson.
Correspondence from Christopher and William Downie and Chris Cottier to the author.

Chapter 19 - Frank George Seaforth Alderson and Cicely Bray (9p&m1/6/P1000).
Biographical notes compiled by FGS Alderson.
Correspondence from Dr Harry Clegg to the author.
Articles in the *Telegraph Magazine* re. Wharram.
Briefing note by the Department of the Environment 1973 re. Wharram.

Index

See Bibliography for ancestor identifier number. The prefix "s" denotes a sibling of.

MORE BOOKS FROM HAYLOFT

The Maddison Line, A Journalist's Journey Around Britain,
Roy Maddison (£10, ISBN 1 904524 06 0)

A Journey of Soles, Lands End to John O'Groats, Kathy Trimmer
(£9.50, ISBN 1 904524 05 2)

The Long Day Done, Mountain Rescue in the Lake District
Jeremy Rowan-Robinson (£9.50, ISBN 1 9045240 4 4)

Odd Corners in Appleby, Gareth Hayes
(£8.50, ISBN 1 9045240 0 1)

The Ghastlies, Trix Jones and Shane Surgey
(£3.99, ISBN 1 9045240 4 4)

Changing the Face of Carlisle, The Life and Times of Percy Dalton, City Engineer and Surveyor, 1926-1949, Marie K. Dickens
(£8, ISBN 0 9540711 9 0)

From Clogs and Wellies to Shiny Shoes, A Windermere Lad's Memories of South Lakeland, Miles R. M. Bolton
(£12.50, ISBN 1 9045240 2 8)

A History of Kaber, Helen McDonald and Christine Dowson,
(£8, ISBN 0 9540711 6 6)

The Gifkin Gofkins, Irene Brenan
(£2.50, ISBN 1 9045240 1 X)

A Dream Come True, the Life and Times of a Lake District National Park Ranger, David Birkett
(£5.50, ISBN 0 9540711 5 8)

Gone to Blazes, Life as a Cumbrian Fireman, David Stubbings
(£9.95, ISBN 0 9540711 4 X)

Changing Times, The Millennium Story of Bolton, Barbara Cotton
(£12.50, ISBN 0 9540711 3 1)

Better by Far a Cumberland Hussar, A History of the Westmorland and Cumberland Yeomanry, Colin Bardgett
(Hardback, £26.95, ISBN 0 9540711 2 3)
(Paperback, £16.95, ISBN 0 9540711 1 5)

Northern Warrior, the Story of Sir Andreas de Harcla, Adrian Rogan
(£8.95, ISBN 0 9523282 8 3)

A Riot of Thorn & Leaf, Dulcie Matthews
(£7.95, ISBN 0 9540711 0 7)

Military Mountaineering, A History of Services Expeditions, 1945-2000,
Retd. SAS Major Bronco Lane
(Hardback, £25.95, ISBN 0 9523282 1 6)
(Paperback, £17.95, ISBN 0 9523282 6 7)

2041 - The Voyage South, Robert Swan
(£8.95, 0 9523282 7 5)

Yows & Cows, A Bit of Westmorland Wit, Mike Sanderson
(£7.95, ISBN 0 9523282 0 8)

Riding the Stang, Dawn Robertson
(£9.99, ISBN 0 9523282 2 4)

Secrets and Legends of Old Westmorland,
Peter Koronka and Dawn Robertson
(Hardback, £17.95, ISBN 0 9523282 4 0)
(Paperback, £11.95, ISBN 0 9523282 9 1)

The Irish Influence, Migrant Workers in Northern England,
Harold Slight
(£4.95, 0 9523282 5 9)

Soldiers and Sherpas, A Taste for Adventure, Brummie Stokes.
(£19.95, 0 9541551 0 6)

North Country Tapestry, Sylvia Mary McCosh
(£10, 0 9518690 0 0)

Pashler's Lane, A Clare Childhood, Elizabeth Holdgate
(£10, 0 9542072 0 3)

Between Two Gardens, The Diary of two Border Gardens,
Sylvia Mary McCosh
(£5.95, 0 9008111 7 X)

Dacre Castle, A short history of the Castle and the Dacre Family,
E. H. A. Stretton
(£5.50, 0 9518690 1 9)

Antarctica Unveiled, Scott's First Expedition and the Quest for the Unknown Continent, David E. Yelverton
(£25.99, 0 8708158 2 2)

You can order any of our books by writing to:
Hayloft Publishing Ltd, South Stainmore,
Stephen, Cumbria, CA17 4EU, UK.
Please enclose a cheque plus £2 for UK postage and packing.
or telephone: +44 (0)17683) 42300
For more information see: www.hayloft.org.uk